THE COMPLETE
HUNTER™

BOWHUNTING
Equipment & Skills

BY
M. R. JAMES
G. FRED ASBELL
DAVE HOLT
DWIGHT SCHUH

Creative Publishing
international

Chanhassen, Minnesota

G. FRED ASBELL, Pope and Young Club President and *Bowhunter* Hunting Editor, began bowhunting in the 1950s. An authority on instinctive shooting, he has written two books and produced a video on the subject.

M. R. JAMES, *Bowhunter* Editor/Founder, Midwesterner by birth and a Montanan by choice, has hunted whitetails and other big game species throughout North America for nearly 40 years. He has been the Editor since *Bowhunter's* initial issue appeared in 1971.

DAVE HOLT, *Bowhunter* Technical Editor, has bowhunted for 40 years. An author and expert on modern bowhunting, he has participated in leading research projects on arrow velocity, kinetic energy and broadhead penetration.

DWIGHT SCHUH, *Bowhunter* Senior Editor, has authored hundreds of articles and nine books including *Fundamentals of Bowhunting* and *Bowhunter's Encyclopedia*. He presents seminars nationwide on big game bowhunting techniques.

Creative Publishing international

President/CEO: Ken Fund
Vice President/Publisher: Linda Ball
Vice President/Retail Sales & Marketing: Kevin Haas

BOWHUNTING EQUIPMENT & SKILLS
By Dwight Schuh, G. Fred Asbell, Dave Holt & M. R. James

Executive Editor, Outdoor Products Group: Don Oster
Book Development Leader and Contributing Writer: David L. Tieszen
Editor: Dave Canfield – *Bowhunter* magazine
Senior Editor: Bryan Trandem
Technical Editors/Advisors: Dave Canfield, M. R. James – *Bowhunter* magazine
Managing Editor: Denise Bornhausen
Copy Editor: Janice Cauley
Associate Creative Director: Brad Springer
Senior Desktop Publishing Specialist: Joe Fahey
Desktop Publishing Specialist: Laurie Kristensen
V.P. Photography and Production: Jim Bindas
Studio Manager: Marcia Chambers
Studio Services Coordinator: Cheryl Neisen
Lead Photographer: William Lindner
Staff Photographers: Mike Hehner, Chuck Nields, Rebecca Schmitt
Photo Assistants: Gretchen Gundersen, Thomas Heck, Mike Hehner, Rob Johnstone, Dave Maas, Andrea Moldzio, Dave Schelitzche, Michael Sipe, Jeff Simpson
Production Manager: Kim Gerber
Production Staff: Dave Austad, Mark Biscan, Laura Hokkanen, Tom Hoops, Mike Schauer, Brent Thomas, Kay Wethern
Cover Photographer: Mark Kayser
Contributing Photographers: Phil Aarrestad, Charles Alsheimer, G. Fred Asbell, Dan Bertalan, Dale C. Spartas/The Green Agency, Chris Kuehn, Stephen W. Maas, Dr. Dave Samuel, Brent Thomas, David L. Tieszen, Joseph L. Tieszen

Contributing Manufacturers: Altier Archery Mfg.; Barrie Archery – Chad Bauman; Bighorn Bowhunting Co.; BrackLynn Products, Inc. – In memory of Kenny Lynn; Carter Enterprises – Jerry Carter; Easton Technical Products, Inc. – Debra W. Adamson; Fine-Line, Inc.; Golden Key Futura, Inc.; Highlander Archery Inc. – Danny Kerley; Hoyt USA – Carla Carden, Jeff Edwards, Sherry Maestas; McKenzie Targets; Mathews, Inc. – Joel Maxfield; Montana Black Gold – Mike Ellig; Mountaineer Archery – Pat Nealis; Muzzy Products Corp.; Neet Products, Inc.; New Archery Products Corp.; Precision Shooting Equipment, Inc. – Terry Greenlund, Dan Hawk; Predator, Inc. – Marc A. Barger; Saunders Archery Co. – Charles Saunders; Scott Archery Manufacturing, Inc.; Sight Master, Inc.; Terry Arrow Rest – Ken Fauser; Zwickey Archery Inc. – Jack Zwickey

Contributing Individuals and Agencies: A.M.O./Archery Manufacturers and Merchants Organization; Bart Biedinger; Bwana Archery – John Larsen, Neil Mellesmoen; Gary Clancy; Compound Doctor – Ron & Muriel Carlson, Keith Edberg, John Landrith; The Farrel Group – Kevin Howard; Hawk Associates – Rich Walton; Chris Kuehn; Eric Lindberg; Jim Lingenfelter; Minnesota Department of Natural Resources – Tyler Quandt, Paul Rice; Outtech, Inc. – Jerry Podratz; Pioneer Research, Inc. – Tyke Arbaugh; Pat & Tom Wagamon

Printed in China
10

The Library of Congress Cataloging-in-Publication Data
Bowhunting equipment & skills / by Dwight Schuh ... [et al.]
     p.   cm. -- (The Complete Hunter)
     Includes index.
     ISBN 0-86573-067-9 (hardcover)
     1. Bowhunting--Equipment and supplies. 2. Archery. I. Schuh, Dwight R. II. Series.
SK36.B677   1997
799.2'15--dc20
                                                    96-35380

Contents

Introduction

Bowhunting. There's nothing like it. Seasons of numbing cold, blazing heat, throbbing muscles, endless hikes and countless frustrations all become worthwhile in one glorious heart-stopping second. A magnificent animal is so close that a single breath or blink of an eye will spook it. It appears – as if by magic – in a spot you've watched for hours. Or it approaches from a distance, giving you time to make ready. It doesn't matter – the thrill's the same, and at this moment it all comes together. It's time for the shot.

In bowhunting, "the shot" actually is the culmination of much more than meets the eye. A bowhunter donning a backpack and vanishing into nature's shadows seems to step into a much less complicated past. We who love the sport cherish its simplicity, but as with any difficult task well done, that "simplicity" only becomes reality after the planning, preparation and practice. In fact, I believe a more accurate description of the bowhunter's relationship with nature would be "pure." If the bowhunter is ready, no experience equals a day in the field. And in this sport, getting there is more than half the fun.

I once was asked where one could learn bowhunting in a weekend seminar. I replied that it's impossible to do so. Properly done, it's a lifetime learning experience. Hunting skills require years of honing and are best developed from an early age. Actual use of archery equipment takes regular training and practice for novice and expert alike. Few beginners can shoot more than 10 or 15 arrows in a session – if they want to be able to move tomorrow. On the other hand, in a good hands-on seminar a person can learn about equipment and how it should be used. As with skiing, golf, fly fishing, swimming and some other sports, a little instruction up front prevents a lifetime of bad habits that come from "winging it."

So here, within the pages of *Bowhunting Equipment & Skills,* is that seminar. Here is what you need to know about the selection and use of bowhunting equipment and development of skills to use it. Here we present the basics for the novice, a valuable reference for the average bowhunter and an excellent review and training aid for the expert.

The primary authors of this book have spent their lifetime involved in bowhunting and are among the sport's best-known authorities. Each of them has made bowhunting history, has written classic books on the sport and continues to pass bowhunting skills and knowledge to the next generation: *Bowhunter's* Founder/Editor M. R. James, Senior Editor Dwight Schuh, Hunting Editor G. Fred Asbell and Technical Editor Dave Holt.

Begin with a general view of bowhunting equipment. You'll see the differences among bow designs and understand the advantages or disadvantages of each. Then the interesting part begins – the accessories. This is where bowhunters become hooked for life and destined to tinker forever among broadheads, fletchings, sights, quivers, gloves, tabs, optics and countless other items, each designed to provide just a little more of an edge.

Armed for the moment with the essentials (there always will be something else beckoning), it's time to tune equipment and sharpen personal skills. The Bowhunting Skills and Tuning sections guide you as you become as one with your equipment.

Now, it's time to bring it all together in the field. Bowhunting offers camaraderie, closeness with nature, solitude and memories. The skill is up to each of us, and it takes a considerable amount. For in the end, it all adds up to one razor-sharp, well-placed broadhead.

Keep 'em sharp!

—*Dave Canfield*
Publisher, *Bowhunter*

This hunter's dream became a reality through planning, preparation and practice

Bowhunting Equipment

Choosing Your Equipment

More than any other style of hunting, bowhunting is more art than science. Just as each archer must adapt a shooting style to fit his or her personality and abilities, the selection of bow and accessories will be a highly personal and subjective choice. Two skilled, expert bowhunters might favor radically different equipment and accessories – partly because of physical differences, but largely because of variations in personal taste.

In an effort to meet the varied needs of bowhunters, manufacturers offer hundreds of different bows and an even greater number of accessories, from carbon shaft arrows to laser sights. Some of these products are passing fads, while others represent important new technology. Each hunter must decide which gadgets are of value.

A hunter need not buy the most expensive bows and accessories, but it does make sense to invest in high-quality equipment. Listen to the advice of bowhunters you respect, and purchase your equipment from reputable sources. Test equipment in the store, if possible.

CHOOSING a bow and bowhunting accessories is largely a matter of personal taste. Some bowhunters eagerly make use of the most modern compound bows and all the latest accessories (left). Others prefer more traditional bows and use accessories sparingly (above).

Personal Variables

No matter what bow style you choose – compound or traditional – before buying a bow you must determine three personal variables: eye dominance, length of draw and draw weight.

EYE DOMINANCE. Bows are configured in right- and left-handed models, and your choice is based on *eye dominance*. Just as most people are either right-handed or left-handed, they generally also have a dominant, or master, eye. In most cases, hand and eye dominance match, but occasionally a right-handed person will have a dominant left eye, or vice versa.

To determine your dominant eye, point at a distant object with both eyes open. Now close your left eye. If your finger still appears to be pointing at the object, you have a dominant right eye. But if your finger appears to shift to the side when you close your left eye, then you have a dominant left eye. For confirmation, point again with both eyes open, then close your

How to Determine Eye Dominance

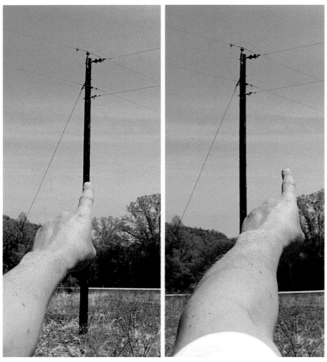

POINT at a distant object with both eyes open (left). Now close your left eye, then your right. When you look through your dominant eye, your finger will still appear to point at the object, but when you look through your subordinate eye, your finger will appear to shift to the side (right).

right eye. If, while you look with your left eye only, your finger still points at the target, you have confirmed that your left eye is dominant.

If your eye dominance matches your hand dominance, simply choose a bow configured for that side. A right-hander with a dominant right eye, for example, should choose a right-handed bow.

If, however, your hand and eye dominance are mismatched, it is best to choose a bow based on eye dominance rather than your hand dominance. A right-hander may at first feel clumsy shooting a left-handed bow, but in the long run he'll shoot better and more comfortably. Research shows that most successful archers sight with the dominant eye, regardless of hand dominance, probably because they can aim with both eyes open, which gives better depth perception and a feel for the target. To aim with the weaker eye, you must close the dominant eye.

DRAW LENGTH. The length of your arms and the width of your shoulders determine your *draw length* – the distance between the bowstring and the grip, when you hold a bow at full draw. Draw length is a specific measurement that governs bow selection and should not be confused with arrow length. Arrows can be, and often are, shorter or longer than your draw length.

A salesman at a sporting goods store can measure your draw length, or you can enlist the aid of a bowhunting

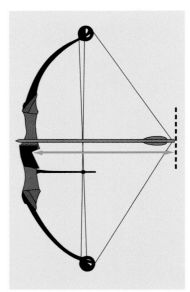

DRAW LENGTH is measured along the arrow from the nock to the point where the arrow intersects the pressure point of the bow handle. Archery manufacturers recommend adding an additional 1¾ inches to this measurement to allow for the width of the riser.

friend. First, nock an arrow onto the bowstring and draw the bow. As you hold comfortably at full draw, have your assistant mark the arrow directly above the pressure point of the handle – a spot that should be even with the arrow-rest hole in the sight window.

Now add 1¾ inches to that measurement to determine your draw length for a compound bow, as specified by the Archery Manufacturers and Merchants

Organization (AMO). If, for example, the measurement is 28 inches from the string to the pressure point at full draw, your draw length would be 29¾ inches.

Most bows allow for large draw length adjustments – from 29 to 31 inches, or from 30 to 32 inches, for example. But if your bow still doesn't match your draw length, you can make additional adjustments by twisting or untwisting the string to change the draw length by up to ¼ inch. On bows with synthetic cables, you can twist the cables tighter to increase draw length, or untwist them to decrease draw length. A combination of twisting or untwisting cables and strings gives a virtually unlimited range of precise draw lengths. Keep in mind, however, that twisting the cables can throw the bow out of tune. Many bows with metal cables have slotted yokes that allow for ¼-inch draw length changes. Remember, though, that these adjustments will alter draw weight as well as draw length. Lengthening the string increases draw weight, shortening the string reduces draw weight, and exactly the opposite is true for lengthening and shortening the cables.

DRAW WEIGHT. Your choice of bows also is governed by the peak *draw weight* – the maximum amount of weight needed to draw the bow. It is impossible to prescribe an exact formula for assigning draw weight, because it varies according to each person's build and body strength. As a broad guideline, however, you should be able to draw your bow easily. If you have to raise a bow over your head for leverage when drawing, it is too heavy. You should be able to repeatedly hold the sights on target and draw the string straight back without straining or shaking.

Remember that shooting on the hunt is much different from shooting at the target range. Drawing smoothly becomes increasingly difficult as fatigue, cold and tension take their toll on your body. If you have to strain to draw a bow in practice, you may find that you can't draw it at all under tough hunting conditions. Choose a bow with a draw weight you can easily handle under any circumstances.

Ensuring a smooth draw isn't the only reason for choosing a bow of reasonable draw weight. Many archers suffer severe, chronic shoulder and elbow injuries, including tendonitis and bursitis, from shooting bows with heavy draw weights over a period of years. These overuse injuries can occur from repeatedly drawing a bow at any draw weight, but the added strain of heavy draw weight can aggravate the problems greatly.

Drawing and holding excessive weight also can contribute to target panic, the bane of many archers (p. 102). And a heavy draw weight, particularly

when coupled with ultralight arrows, sends destructive vibrations through a bow. Although improvements in modern bows have greatly reduced breakage problems, the greater the stress on a bow, the greater the potential for damage.

Generally speaking, many modern compound bows in the 60-pound class are heavy enough for all North American game animals. Any weight above that may give your arrows a flatter trajectory, which can be a benefit at unknown distances, but it doesn't significantly improve penetration. In truth, it is kinetic energy (p. 118) – not a bow's poundage, that matters most.

How do you determine your comfortable draw weight? Test several bows of differing draw weights, and choose one you can draw easily. If you can easily draw 70 pounds, then select a comparable bow, but most shooters are more comfortable with a 50- to 60-pound bow. Wheel design will greatly affect the amount of weight a shooter can comfortably draw.

KINETIC ENERGY is more important than draw weight when choosing a bow for hunting.

Compound Bows

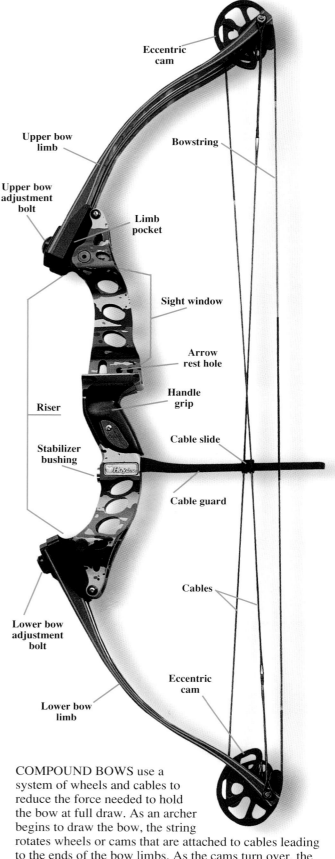

The vast majority of hunters use compound bows that incorporate cams and cables to reduce by 50 to 80 percent the force needed to hold the bow at full draw. This *let-off* allows you to hold a compound bow much longer at full draw than you could hold a comparable longbow or recurve. For example, a compound bow with a 60-pound draw weight and 50 percent let-off requires only 30 pounds of pull to hold at full draw. A 60-pound longbow, by contrast, requires a full 60 pounds of force. The let-off percentage is important when choosing a bow. Keep in mind, however, that some states do not allow bows with a let-off greater than 65 percent, and that the Pope and Young Club record book will not accept animals taken with bows listed with a let-off greater than 65 percent.

A compound bow is a sophisticated, intricate piece of equipment. To make an informed choice, you'll need to understand each component, as well as design variations.

Wheels

Compound bows can be categorized by the number and shape of the wheels that hold the cables and string. Since the early 1980s, most compound bow designs have featured two irregularly shaped wheels, or *cams*. The two-cam design is still the most popular, but since the early 1990s, the one-cam design has gained major popularity. One-cam bows feature a single, eccentrically shaped cam on the bottom limb and a perfectly round control wheel, called an *idler*, on the top. Virtually all manufacturers now offer their bows in both one- and two-cam versions. The only other notable deviation from the two-cam design is the lever-action bow, in which the cams are built into the riser rather than positioned on the tips of the limbs (opposite page).

Eccentric cam

Upper bow limb

Bowstring

Upper bow adjustment bolt

Limb pocket

Sight window

Arrow rest hole

Handle grip

Riser

Cable slide

Stabilizer bushing

Cable guard

Cables

Lower bow adjustment bolt

Eccentric cam

Lower bow limb

COMPOUND BOWS use a system of wheels and cables to reduce the force needed to hold the bow at full draw. As an archer begins to draw the bow, the string rotates wheels or cams that are attached to cables leading to the ends of the bow limbs. As the cams turn over, the cables apply leverage that helps flex the bow's limbs. The result is that an archer can hold a bow at full draw using as little as 20 percent of the full draw weight.

ONE-CAM BOWS. The biggest selling point for one-cam bows is that wheel synchronization is unnecessary, since there is only a single cam. On two-cam bows, by contrast, the cams must be synchronized to rotate at the same rate to prevent the string from jerking up and down during the power stroke, sending the arrow out in an erratic oscillation. On one-cam designs, the idler wheel uses a two-track design that ensures that the nock of the arrow will travel in a straight line when the string is released.

TWO-CAM BOWS. Generally speaking, you can choose from three different wheel designs on standard two-cam compound bows. In the early days of compound bows, manufacturers offered bows with perfectly round wheels, but today these have largely been replaced with irregularly shaped wheels, known as cams. The outside edge of each cam has two tracks – one for the bowstring, the other for a cable. The cams can be categorized as soft, medium or hard, depending on their shape and design.

Soft cams, sometimes called *energy wheels*, have a round lobe on the string side of the wheel and an oval-shaped lobe on the cable side. The round string lobe gives a very smooth draw, while the oval cable lobe gives more speed and power than a fully round lobe. Soft cams store roughly one foot-pound (fp) of energy per pound of draw weight. This means that a 60-pound bow stores 60 fp of energy.

Medium cams have oval lobes on both the string and cable sides. These wheels still allow for a relatively smooth draw, but they offer more energy storage and speed than soft cams. Medium cams store about 1.2 fp of energy for each pound of peak weight: thus, a 60-pound bow stores 72 fp of energy.

Hard cams have a severely elliptical shape, which is the reason they are often called *hatchet cams*. These cams may store 1.3 to 1.4 fp of energy per pound of peak draw weight, and are thus the fastest of all the cam styles.

CHOOSING A DESIGN. You might assume that hard cams are the best choice, since they allow the bow to store more energy and thus deliver faster arrow speed, flatter trajectory and greater penetration. But the extra energy offered by hard cams doesn't come without a price. The *draw-force curve* (p. 14) shows the differences between drawing and holding a soft-cam and hard-cam bow.

With soft cams, the force required to draw the bow builds gradually, peaks out sharply, then tapers off gradually before reaching a *valley* – the point where the holding weight is reduced. With hard cams, the draw force increases sharply, extends for several

DESIGN VARIATIONS for compound bows include the standard two-cam (opposite page), the single-cam (left) and lever-action bow (right). One-cam bows have a single energy cam on the bottom and a perfectly round idler wheel on the top.

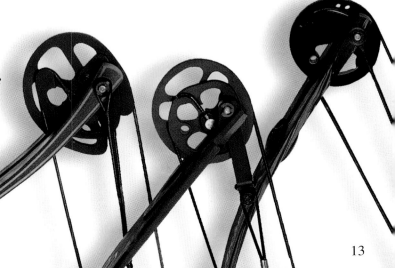

CAM VARIATIONS include the *soft cam* (right), *medium cam* (center) and *hard cam*, sometimes called a *hatchet cam* (left).

13

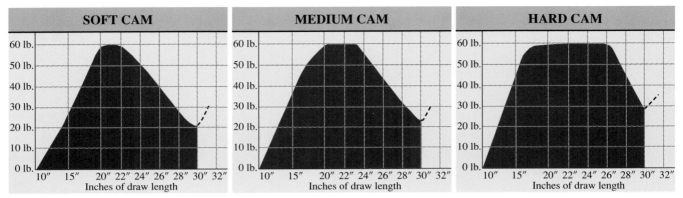

SOFT CAM	MEDIUM CAM	HARD CAM

Draw-force curves for soft-cam (left), medium-cam (center) and hard-cam bows (right)

inches at peak weight, then drops off acutely to a short valley. Medium cams fall somewhere between these two extremes. Thus, a hard-cam bow requires greater strength to draw initially, and many have a tendency to jerk as the draw suddenly drops into the valley.

Although hard cams provide greater arrow speed than do soft cams, many hunters find them more difficult to use, for several reasons. First, hard cams have a short valley, less than 1 inch in length. This requires that the hunter hold at full draw with great precision; the slightest bit of creep before the shot can significantly alter the arrow's point of impact.

Hard-cam bows generally have a shorter *brace height* – the measured distance from the string to the bow handle before the bow is drawn. A short brace height lengthens the power stroke of the string, which increases arrow speed, but it also gives the

arrow less time to straighten out as it leaves the string and passes the arrow rest.

Increased speed can also cause problems. Faster arrows tend to be more temperamental than slower arrows, because slight flaws in the release are exaggerated by high velocity.

Finally, hard-cam bows are often noisier than soft-cams, because they transmit a larger percentage of their energy into the handle and limbs, creating sound-producing vibrations. Adding a stabilizer can help absorb some of this vibration, but a hard-cam bow is rarely as silent as a soft-cam model.

An experienced archer who demands raw speed and who knows how to tune and maintain a high-performance bow may prefer hard cams. For longer shots at unknown distances, the added speed does

BRACE HEIGHT is the distance between the string and the bow handle. A short brace height (left) gives the arrow less time to straighten out as it leaves the string and clears the arrow rest. A longer brace height (right) is inherently more accurate than a short brace height.

offer an advantage. But the average bowhunter facing typical 20- to 30-yard shots at white-tailed deer will probably be happier with a soft-cam or medium-cam bow, which is quiet, smooth-shooting and easy to tune.

DRAW-LENGTH ADJUSTMENT. Modern cams offer several options for adjusting draw length. One version, known as an E-wheel, has three string pegs, and draw length is adjusted by moving the string to a different peg. On other bows, the draw length is altered by changing string modules on the wheels.

These two methods of changing draw length have a similar effect on draw weight – that is, increasing draw length also increases draw weight, and decreasing draw length reduces draw weight. On another style of cam, you can rotate a built-in string module to alter draw length without affecting draw weight.

LET-OFF. The cams on a compound bow are essentially pulleys that allow you to hold the bow at full draw using less force than the full draw weight. This reduction in drawing force is known as let-off, and is determined by the design of the cams.

At one time, 50 percent let-off was considered maximum, but you can now choose bows with a let-off as high as 80 percent. For example, on an 80-pound bow with 80 percent let-off, you are holding only 16 pounds at full draw. Reducing the holding weight does, however, also reduce stored energy and speed. And hunters who release with fingers sometimes have difficulty releasing smoothly on a bow with very low holding weight.

For most hunters, a bow with 60 or 65 percent let-off is a good compromise. With some compound bows, you can change the let-off by putting the cam axle in a different hole; on other bows, you can change modules on the cams.

Variations for Draw-length Adjustment

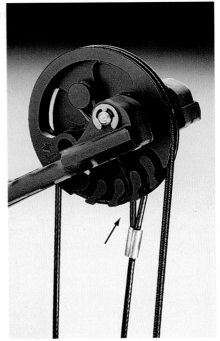

MOVE THE LOOP on the end of the string to a different peg on the cam (arrow). Two-cam bows will have adjustment pegs on both cams.

MOVE THE STRING to a different slot (arrow), leaving the loop attached to the single peg on the cam. On two-cam bows, there will be slots on both cams.

Modular Adjustment Systems

ROTATE MODULES. On some bow styles with rotating cam modules, loosening the mounting screws (arrow) and rotating the modules changes the draw length or let-off percentage of the bow.

CHANGE MODULES. Depending on the make of the bow, changing cam modules (inset) will adjust either the draw length of the bow or the amount of let-off.

Riser

The center portion of a compound bow, called the *riser*, provides a hand grip, anchor points for the bow limbs and mounting holes for the arrow rest, cable guard, over-draw and sights. At one time, wood was the standard material for bow risers, chosen for its warm feel and beauty. But wood has virtually disappeared from the compound bow market, replaced by various forms of metal or carbon. For years now, die-cast magnesium has dominated the handle market by virtue of its light weight, reasonable cost and durability.

However, the manufacturing process can create two notable imperfections in cast handles. First, when molten metal is poured into a mold, tiny bubbles form which can create a weak spot. Magnesium handles have been known to break, especially when high draw weights are combined with light arrows. Second, a cast-metal handle tends to warp as it cools, which can erode tolerances enough to affect the performance of the bow.

RISER MATERIALS INCLUDE: (1) magnesium, (2) forged aluminum, (3) machined aluminum and (4) carbon.

For these reasons, machined aluminum handles have begun to capture much of the market. Since these handles are lathed from a solid aluminum billet, they have precise tolerances and are extremely strong. However, machined aluminum handles are generally heavier than magnesium, and they're somewhat more expensive.

A new version is the forged/machined aluminum handle riser. In this process, an aluminum billet is first compressed into a handle-shaped mold and is then machined to add the finishing touches. Manufacturers say that forged handles are stronger than those machined from a billet, so handles can be made slimmer and lighter without sacrificing strength.

Carbon handle risers are finding their place, as well. The benefit here is light weight. Some carbon bows weigh as little as 3 pounds when fully equipped with overdraw, sight and quiver. For backcountry hunting, where an archer has to pack a bow up and down mountains all day, ultralight carbon handle risers should gain a solid following.

Riser types include (1) deflexed, (2) straight and (3) reflexed

BALANCE is better on bows with reflexed and straight risers than on those with deflexed handles. With a reflexed handle (above) the bow generally remains upright or tips forward when the bow hand is relaxed. With a deflexed handle (inset), the bow often tips back, unless it is equipped with a stabilizer.

HANDLE DESIGN. Handles come in three basic shapes – straight, reflexed and deflexed (above). On straight handles, the limb pockets at the top and bottom of the riser lie in direct line with the handle. On deflexed bows, the limb pockets lie behind the handle (that is, closer to the string), and on reflexed bows, the limb pockets extend in front of the handle.

As a general rule, bows with straight and reflexed handles have a lower brace height than bows with deflexed handles, and are thus faster. Some highly reflexed bows have brace heights of 6 inches or less, compared to straight bows with brace heights of 7 to 8 inches, and strongly deflexed bows with brace heights up to 10 inches.

Bows with a low brace height are faster because they have a longer power stroke. A bow with a 30-inch draw length and 6-inch brace height, for example, has a power stroke 4 inches longer than a comparable bow with a 10-inch brace height (right). With a 4-inch-longer power stroke, the bow with the lower brace height will shoot significantly faster.

The obvious benefit of a reflexed riser, then, is greater arrow speed. Reflexed and straight bows

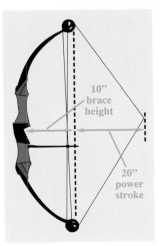

Power stroke

also have good balance; after the shot they will stand straight up in your hand or tip forward without the use of a stabilizer. But the low brace height of a reflexed bow can also reduce the stability of the arrow, since it has less time to straighten out in the time between leaving the string and clearing the arrow rest. A low brace height can also preclude the use of a long overdraw, because the cables may strike the back of the overdraw when the arrow is shot.

Deflexed bows, with their higher brace height, are popular because they are more forgiving. The higher brace height contributes by giving arrows plenty of room to straighten out as the nock leaves the string and passes through the arrow rest. Since deflexed

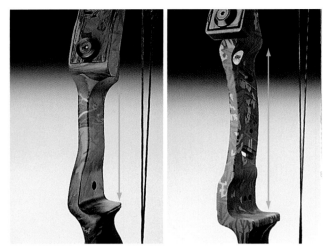

SIGHT WINDOW on short axle-to-axle bow (left) and long axle-to-axle bow (right).

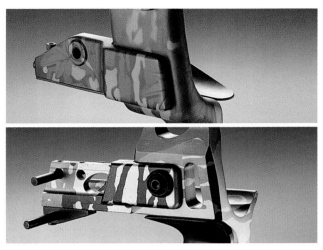

CHOOSE a bow with an overdraw if you have a long draw length or are seeking higher arrow speeds. Both built-in overdraws (top) and dovetail-type overdraws (bottom) are strong and quiet.

bows tend to tip back in the hand after each shot, most archers use a stabilizer to improve balance.

Nearly all bows now use a cutout handle design. It was first developed for use with overdraws to ensure that broadheads would safely clear the riser, but it has advantages for all shooters. The cutout (below) allows you to safely pull a broadhead back all the way to the rest, providing a short overdraw effect. It also gives you lots of lee-way in adjusting center shot, and assures good fletching clearance for even the biggest vanes.

Directly above the broad-head cutout area is the *sight window* through which the archer aims. Generally, the shorter the overall length of the bow, the shorter the sight win-dow. If your peep sight (p. 56) is 6 inches or more above the nocking

Cutout area on the riser

point, make sure to buy a bow with a sight window greater than 6 inches high; a shorter window will obscure your top sight pins. If you anchor high, which moves your peep down, you can manage with a sight window shorter than 6 inches.

If you have a particularly long draw length, consider choosing a bow with a handle that is channeled to accept dedicated overdraw brackets. Other bows have handles with an overdraw built directly into the handle – a very solid, quiet design.

GRIP. The grip portion of the riser varies widely from bow to bow. Some have big, meaty grips; others are much slimmer. Try several to find a grip that fits your hand and feels natural. Some bowhunters find that thick grips lead to erratic shooting, because with more hand on the grip, there is a greater tendency to twist, or *torque,* the riser. And it is difficult to dupli-cate the same hand position for each shot.

Some hunters even remove the plastic or wood grip entirely and shoot without it. To make the handle warmer and more comfortable without the grip, these archers wrap the handle with leather, fleece or base-ball-bat tape (below).

Bow handle with grip removed

RECURVED LIMBS (top) and STRAIGHT LIMBS (bottom) vary little in the way that they perform.

Limbs

At one time, all good compound bows featured laminated wood limbs, and only cheaper models had solid fiberglass limbs. No so today. Now, most high-performance bows have limbs made from molded or laminated fiberglass. They are virtually impervious to heat, moisture and other problems that threatened wood limbs.

Some laminated bow limbs incorporate layers of carbon as well as fiberglass. Carbon improves the performance of very thin limbs by acting as a stiffener. This allows the limbs to be made narrower or thinner without sacrificing strength.

Some bows feature recurved limbs, others use straight limbs (above). Recurved limbs may have more eye appeal, but in terms of performance, you'll see little difference.

Cables and Strings

Early compound bows had Dacron® strings and metal cables. Some companies still use steel cables, but virtually all have replaced Dacron strings with Fast Flight® or other synthetic materials. And most manufacturers have adopted totally synthetic rigging, replacing metal cables with string cables. By reducing weight and stretch, these systems have increased arrow speed 8 to 10 feet per second. Using synthetic materials has also simplified bow tuning.

Early Fast Flight systems had a poor reputation because stretching of the strings and cables constantly changed the tune of the bow. Fast Flight does stretch to some degree, but the major problem with early strings was not stretch but *creep* – slippage under the end servings. Improved manufacturing techniques have eliminated that problem, and today's Fast Flight riggings are very stable.

In an effort to totally eliminate string and cable stretch, some manufacturers began to use a material called Vectran®, which does not stretch. But Vectran frays easily, an obvious shortcoming on hunting bows, and it can break after a few thousand shots.

Seeking the best of both worlds, string makers have combined Fast Flight with Vectran to make durable, low-stretch string materials, called *450 Premium®* and *S4®*. Most bows today use one of these materials, or Fast Flight, for their strings and cables.

A convenient innovation is the *split cable yoke* (right), a feature that reduces wheel lean and makes it possible to tune the bow without a bow press.

The cable guard, which holds the cable to the side to prevent fletching contact with the cables, comes standard on all compound bows. The adjustable rod should be offset just enough for complete clearance between the cables and fletching, but it should not stretch the cables any farther to the side than necessary, or excessive wheel lean could result.

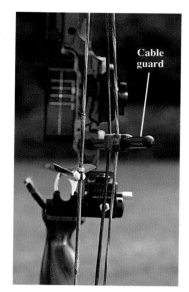

Cable guard

Bow Length

As manufacturers seek to improve maneuverability and increase speed, compound bows gradually have grown shorter. Average bow length is now under 40 inches (measured axle to axle), and most manufacturers now make some models in the 34-inch range.

Axle-to-axle measurement

Physical Weight

The physical weight of a bow makes little difference if you plan to spend all your time in a tree stand. But if you'll be climbing western mountains day after day, a fully equipped 6- or 7- pound bow could become a burden. Some new carbon-handle bows weigh as low as 3 pounds, and slim-line aluminum bows are down near 4 pounds (without accessories).

Shorter bows generally are faster than longer bows. For a given draw length, the wheels on short bows are bigger than on longer bows, which increases the wheel speed. It's a matter of leverage, like using a short-handled wrench (small wheel) compared to a long-handled wrench (big wheel). Archers with a short draw length, say under 28 inches, gain more speed from this principle than do those with longer draw lengths.

As always, you don't get something for nothing. Many archers agree a short bow is more subject to hand torque than a longer bow. If you're an experienced archer well versed in the arts of tuning and shooting, you can enjoy the benefits of a short bow. But if you're just learning, or don't have time to perfect your tackle and form, a short, fast bow may be more of a handicap than a help.

Short bows are not well suited to archers who release with fingers, primarily because the acute string angle at full draw pinches the fingers (below). The severity of the finger pinch depends on draw length, of

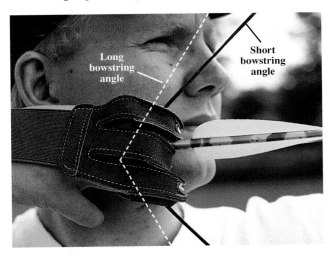

course, but it's fairly safe to say you'll have better success using a release aid with bows shorter than 40 inches. Finger shooters generally stay in the 43- to 44-inch draw-length range.

Speed

Bows are rated by the AMO for a certain speed: the velocity of a 30-inch, 540-grain arrow shot at 60 pounds. The AMO ratings let you compare the relative speed of different bows, but high speed ratings don't necessarily mean superior performance. High arrow speed is good up to a point, but it has its limits. Generally, these recommendations point to a maximum arrow speed of 265 feet per second. Beyond that, the potential for poor arrow flight and bow damage increase dramatically.

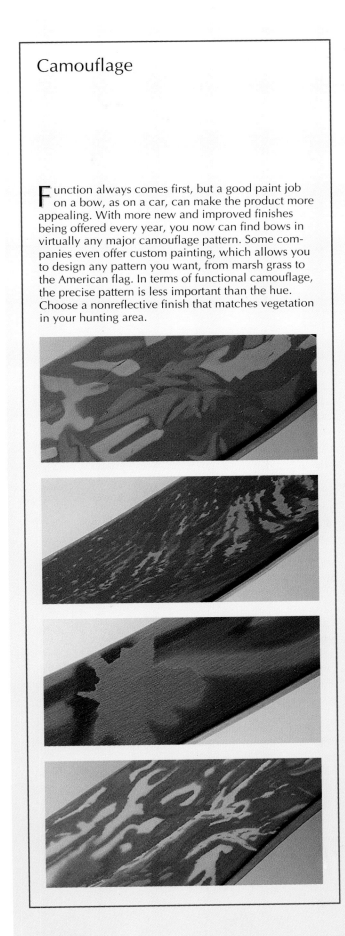

Camouflage

Function always comes first, but a good paint job on a bow, as on a car, can make the product more appealing. With more new and improved finishes being offered every year, you now can find bows in virtually any major camouflage pattern. Some companies even offer custom painting, which allows you to design any pattern you want, from marsh grass to the American flag. In terms of functional camouflage, the precise pattern is less important than the hue. Choose a nonreflective finish that matches vegetation in your hunting area.

Bow Care & Maintenance

Like any fine hunting weapon, your bow needs to be treated with care and will require periodic maintenance. Heat can damage any bow, whether it is wood, fiberglass or a carbon composite. Never store a bow in the trunk of a car or carry it in a gun rack that is exposed to direct sunlight.

Over time, mud and rain can gum up the axles on a bow to the point of increasing draw weight and reducing arrow speed. To prevent this problem, oil the axles and wheels after every few days in the field, using a light machine oil or a Teflon®-based lubricant. Some companies make nonscented oils for just this purpose.

Bowstrings and synthetic cables eventually fray from rubbing against branches and other abrasive surfaces. To reduce fraying, regularly lubricate the string and cables with a liberal coat of string wax or beeswax.

If you nick a string with a broadhead or see visible fraying, replace it immediately. For this purpose, you should always carry a spare bowstring in the field, set up exactly like the one on your bow. Along with the spare string, carry a simple bow press (opposite page). With some bows, you can use an allen wrench to relax the bow limbs enough to change the string.

Never dry-fire a bow. When a bow is fired, the arrow absorbs as much as 80 percent of the energy released by the limbs, sending only 20 percent into the bow itself. If you dry-fire a bow by shooting it with no arrow on the string – the bow itself absorbs 100 percent of the energy, and the stress of vibration through the limbs, handle, cables and string can blow your bow apart. Many unfortunate beginners have been injured by dry-firing a bow.

Shooting excessively light arrows can produce a similar effect, because light arrows absorb a small percentage of the bow's energy. To be safe, always adhere to the AMO guidelines for arrow selection (p. 36).

USE a double-pull, also called two-point, bow press when relaxing your bow. A single-pull press may damage your bow.

Bow Care Tips

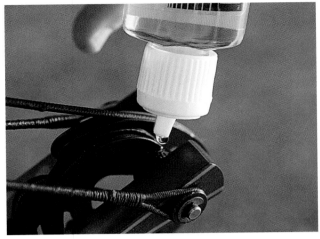

OIL axles every few days when in the field.

AVOID smearing insect repellents on the surface of your bow. The chemicals in these products can ruin the finish.

CARRY an extra bowstring prepared for your bow and a portable bow press when in the field.

CARRY a set of allen wrenches in your tackle box, and check for loose parts before shooting or hunting.

INSPECT the bowstring before shooting; frayed strings should be replaced.

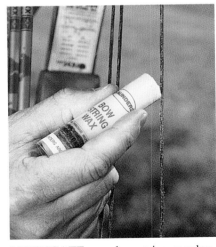

LUBRICATE your bowstring regularly with beeswax or a commercial bowstring wax.

KEEP your bow away from heat. Laminated bow limbs can come apart after only a few hours in a hot vehicle.

Bow Storage Tips

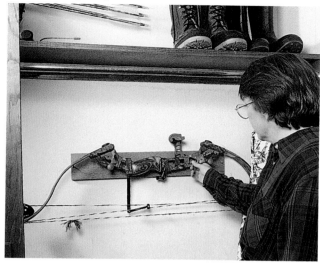

STORE your bow in a cool, dry area out of direct sunlight. Never store it hanging by the string or cables. Hang your bow by the riser, lay it on a flat surface, or store it in a bow holder.

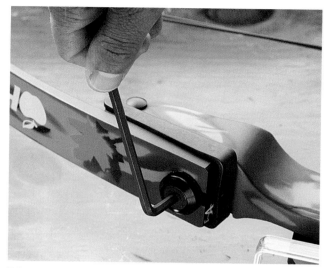

RELAX the tension on the string and cables by backing out the limb bolts before storing your bow for the season.

How to Replace a String Using a Portable Bow Press

INSERT a rod through the V in each of the limbs. Place a protective pad under each cable in the Vs, if desired. Adjust the jackscrew out 1 inch. Pull the cable tight through the slotted rod, making sure that it is secure in each end.

TURN the jackscrew to relieve pressure on the string and cables; then replace the string. Relax the press by loosening the jackscrew, making sure the string and cables are in the proper position on the cams.

Re-Serving a Bowstring

The area of the string where the arrow nock fits is wrapped with nylon monofilament, Fast Flight or Spectra™. This reinforced area, called *serving*, protects the string against wear. If the serving breaks or comes unraveled, or if your arrow nocks fit too tightly or loosely on the string, you may need to re-serve the string. If you have trouble making the whip-finish described opposite, practice the technique with a wooden dowel and a rope or string.

How to Re-serve a Bowstring

(1) SERVE a bowstring from well above the arrow rest to well below the arrow rest.

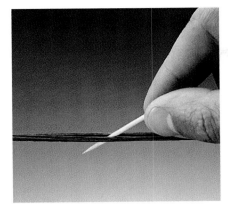

(2) SEPARATE the strands of the bowstring at the point you want the serving to start, using a toothpick or awl.

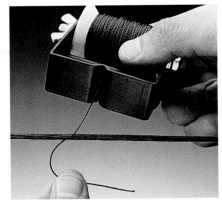

(3) INSERT the end of the new serving thread through the string.

(4) BEGIN wrapping the serving down around the string, securing the loose end of the serving. If you shoot right-handed, wrap the serving around the thread in a clockwise direction; if left-handed, wrap the thread counterclockwise.

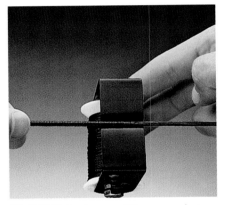

(5) KEEP the loops of the wrapping tight against one another, but not so tight that it can cut strands on the bowstring. Now draw out a large loop of thread, keeping tension of serving string. Cut serving off tool.

(6) BEGIN wrapping the bowstring inside the loop, back toward the served portion. Circle the string at least 10 times, wrapping in the opposite direction from the rest of the serving.

(7) CONTINUE wrapping the serving around the bowstring, pinching the free end of the serving thread against the string. As you wind the bottom of the serving loop around the string, the top of the loop will unwind.

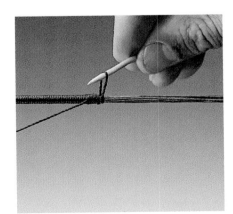

(8) HOLD the final loop tight with a toothpick when all the serving thread is wrapped snug against the string, then pull on the end of the thread to draw the loop tight against the string.

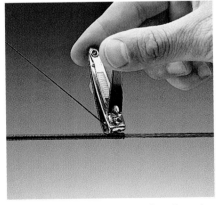

(9) CLIP off the loose serving thread flush with the wrapped serving, using a fingernail clipper.

Recurves & Longbows

One of the fastest-growing segments of bowhunting today is traditional archery. Traditional equipment – longbows and recurved bows, commonly called *recurves*, all but disappeared in the 1970s with the appearance and rise to popularity of the compound bow. But in the 1980s, interest in traditional "stick bows" was reborn – modestly at first, but gradually gaining a respectable following. Today, the stick bow movement shows no signs of slowing down.

The hunter who carries a recurve or longbow typically is an experienced archer who has mastered the modern compound and is looking for an additional challenge. Some choose stick bows for aesthetic reasons; recurves and longbows are simple and beautiful, without the mechanical gadgetry that clutters a compound bow. Instinctive shooters are also drawn to traditional bows for their light weight and smooth draw.

But be aware that traditional bows are more difficult to use. They cannot be tuned and sighted with the same precision as compound bows, and they require more force to hold at

TRADITIONAL BOWS, sometimes called *stick bows*, can be divided into two styles. On a *recurve bow* (left) the limbs sweep back toward the bowstring, then angle back toward the front of the bow. A *longbow* (right) has limbs with a single power curve angling back toward the bowstring.

full draw. A 60-pound longbow reaches 60 pounds at full draw with no let-off, while a comparable compound bow with 50 percent let-off requires only 30 pounds of holding force.

The differences between a recurve and longbow are obvious to the eye. Recurve bows have limbs that curve back toward the front of the bow; most longbows have limbs that form a smooth curve toward the string. Which type do you choose? It's mostly a matter of personal preference. The recurve is probably the best choice for an archer already familiar with modern compound bows. Except for the let-off feature, the compound bow and the recurve are very similar. Both are medium-length bows with pistol-style grips and have comparable performance. With practice, proficiency with a recurve is easily attainable for those making the transition from modern equipment.

The longbow closely resembles the classic bow used by Native Americans and medieval archers. Although it is pleasurable to shoot, the longbow is a more difficult transition for a compound bow hunter. The longbow is extremely light for shooters conditioned to modern compound tackle, and the handle style is very different. Most shooters first gain experience with a recurve before turning to the longbow. Many traditionalists enjoy shooting both types of stick bows.

Traditional Bows Built by Traditional Craftsmen

Although some manufacturers offer a variety of traditional recurves and longbows, which can be purchased through standard archery shop outlets, much of the traditional equipment available today is built by individual bowyers in small shops.

A small bowmaker can give you the personal attention necessary to tailor a bow to your exact needs. But remember that small businesses appear and disappear with regularity. Before you buy any traditional bow, find out as much about the manufacturer as possible. How long has he been in business? How many bows has he built? What type of warranty does he offer? Does he build the bows himself, or does he contract the work out to others?

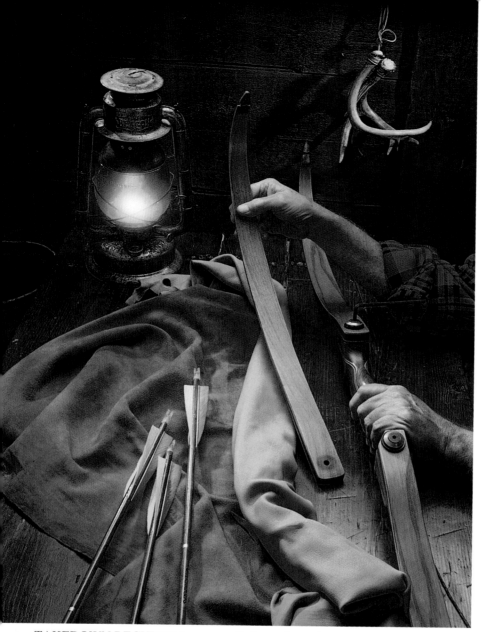

Draw length	Bow length
27 inches or less	56 or 58 inches
28 to 29 inches	60 or 62 inches
29 to 30 inches	62 or 64 inches
more than 30 inches	64 or 66 inches

58 inches are typically for specialty uses, or for shooters with shorter draw lengths. Bows over 64 inches are preferred by shooters with draw lengths exceeding 30 inches. Because of the limb design, a short recurve is more comfortable to shoot than a short longbow.

When choosing a recurve bow, match the bow length to your individual draw length, as shown in the general recommendations chart above.

When choosing a bow length, consider your personal preferences and how you will use the bow. Bowhunting in open country or by stalking will allow the use of a longer bow. Tree-stand hunters often prefer a shorter bow, as do those hunting thick cover. Some archers prefer the feel and comfort of a longer bow; others like the balance and maneuverability of a shorter bow.

TAKEDOWN RECURVE bows usually have three pieces. The length of the bow and its draw weight can be changed by attaching different limbs to the riser. The one-piece recurve has a more traditional look than a takedown. Though less popular than takedown bows, the one-piece recurve is lighter and has better balance.

Recurve Bows

Today's recurve bow is fast, quiet, stable and a pleasure to shoot. Each limb on the recurve has two power curves that bend as the bow is drawn. This gives the recurve more potential energy and faster speed than the typical longbow, which has a single power curve on each limb. Some recurve bows are comparable to compound bows in speed. And the recurve draws smoother and has less hand shock than the longbow.

LENGTH. Recurved hunting bows come in a wide range of lengths, from 46 to 72 inches, but the most popular lengths are 60 and 62 inches. Bows below

DESIGN. Recurves are available in solid one-piece style or in takedown models. One-piece bows have a fixed length and bow weight, while takedown recurves consist of three pieces – two limbs and a riser section.

One-piece bows have a more traditional appearance that some hunters prefer, and they generally are lighter and have better balance than takedown bows. But the takedown recurve is considerably more versatile. By changing limbs on a takedown bow, you can alter its length and draw weight – a distinct advantage, especially for an archer just beginning to use a recurve. A newcomer who begins with a

SIGHT WINDOW LENGTH can vary dramatically from one bow to another (right).

Sight window

64-inch, 50-pound bow, for example, may decide after a year or two that a 62-inch, 55-pound bow is more appropriate. Rather than buy a new bow, the archer can simply purchase a new set of limbs and mount them on the original riser.

RISER. The length of the riser is a major factor in the length of the sight window, and, in combination with the limbs, is basic to the design and feel of the bow.

Some hunters prefer a longer riser section because it allows a longer sight window, which affords a better view of the target. But a longer riser usually means shorter limbs, which will affect the way the bow feels in the hand when shot. For this reason, many archers prefer the combination of a short riser and longer limbs. If the bow is canted sideways

when shot (above), a longer sight window is not needed. Selecting the right length is best accomplished by shooting many bows with different riser lengths and choosing the one that feels best for your shooting style.

Limbs are usually laminated using fiberglass and a variety of woods. Risers can be made from a wide variety of materials. Some modern recurves have cast or machined aluminum risers, but most have wood risers, either solid or laminated. Wood risers are often customized with inlays. Some risers are designed to be shot with arrow rests, stabilizers and sights, similar to those used on compound bows.

DRAW WEIGHT. It is impossible to overemphasize the importance of selecting a bow that you can draw and shoot comfortably. The most common error when selecting a bow – modern or traditional – is choosing a draw weight that is too heavy. The average man can manage a bow in the 45- to 50-pound range, while women should choose 30 to 35 pounds.

A reasonable draw weight is particularly important when you first begin shooting with a recurve. Beginners can be taught to shoot adequately in a few sessions if they are drawing moderate weight; using bows that are too heavy, they may never learn to shoot correctly.

Longbows

A few years ago, the longbow was an oddity and archers who shot them were few and far between. Today, the longbow is a common sight in hunting camps and on archery ranges all across the country. For many, the longbow represents a return to the original roots of archery in the United States. The native American Indians shot longbows, as did the first archers of note in this century, including Art Young, Saxton Pope, Maurice and Will Thompson, and Chief Compton.

Longbows don't shoot as fast as recurves or compound bows, and they require more practice for an archer to achieve proficiency. They are also rougher in the hand and produce more hand shock. But these primitive characteristics are precisely what devotees of traditional archery find so appealing.

Longbows have other merits. Because they use longer limbs and have limbs with a single curve, longbows are particularly stable bows. They are also very quiet. Many archers find the combination of stability and silence ideal for hunting.

Although today's longbows are mostly built with modern materials, including fiberglass, there is a segment of the longbow fraternity that builds and shoots the *self bow*, which is made entirely of a single piece of wood.

BOW LENGTH. Because the longbow limb is a single power curve – as opposed to the recurve's double curve – the limbs must be longer in order to achieve the necessary efficiency. The most popular longbow lengths are 66 and 68 inches, but modern materials are now making it possible to create 62- and 64-inch longbows that have excellent performance. As tree-stand hunters switch to longbows, shorter bows are likely to become increasingly popular.

As with the recurve, the ideal bow length depends largely on your draw length. Keep in mind that the typical longbow shooter's draw will be about 1 inch less than with a recurve, and about 1 1/2 to 2 inches less than with a compound bow. Draw lengths exceeding 29 1/2 inches are rare in longbow shooters. The draw length recommendations shown opposite

SELF BOWS are longbows fashioned from a single piece of wood. The type of wood used for these beautiful bows depends on the bowyer's personal preferences. Other longbows are laminated (inset) using different types of wood and fiberglass.

are based on an average shooter and a longbow of standard modern design.

DESIGN. Most longbows use a one-piece design. Some two-piece takedown models are offered, but they make up a small portion of the total longbow market. In contrast to the takedown recurve, which is aimed at versatility, the takedown longbow's appeal is mostly a matter of convenience (left) – making the bow shorter.

The limbs on most longbows are a combination of fiberglass and other materials, and there has been much debate among manufacturers as to the best combination of materials. Limbs that incorporate bamboo, maple, yew, osage, black locust, hickory, tamarack and other woods are all available. Although some materials draw easier and some may have less hand shock, in truth, there is little difference in performance. This is because most of the limb power in a longbow comes from the fiberglass, not the wood laminations. In the modern longbow, performance is determined mostly by bow design and construction.

However, self bows, which are made without fiberglass, may be significantly affected by the choice of limb material.

DRAW WEIGHT. Because longbows are slightly less efficient than recurves or compounds, some archers make the mistake of compensating by choosing an overly heavy draw weight. The poor shooting syndrome that results from being overbowed is often blamed on the longbow. As with any bow, select a longbow weight which is comfortable for you and easy to shoot.

Recomendations for Matching Longbow Length to Draw Length

Draw length	Bow length
26 inches or less	66 inches or less
27 to 29 inches	66 inches
more than 29 inches	68 inches or more

Stringing Traditional Bows

At one time, the only way to string a recurve bow or longbow was by bending the limbs inward, either across the leg, or by holding the tip of the bow under the foot and bending the opposite limb downward with one hand while lifting on the riser with the other hand. Both methods were difficult and dangerous, resulting in many twisted limbs and broken bows, and serious archers no longer string their bows in this way.

Instead, recurve bows and longbows are now typically strung using a bowstringer, an inexpensive accessory often included when you purchase a bow. Bowstringers take several different forms, but all allow the bow to be strung without danger to the bow or the shooter. Most consist of a nylon cord with a leather pocket attached to each end. To string the bow, you slide one pocket onto each limb tip, then stand on the middle of the cord while lifting on the riser with one hand. As the limbs bend inward, use your other hand to slide the string into the string grooves on the tip.

BOWSTRINGER makes easy work of stringing a recurve bow or longbow.

WARNING. Never try to string a bow by bending it over your knee or holding the tip with your foot. These methods are likely to damage the bow or cause injury.

Arrows & Heads

L ike good bullets, arrows are the link between you and the game you're hunting. You have control over the bow until the time of the release, but then the arrow is on its own and the entire outcome of your hunt depends on the flight of that arrow. So you want the most accurate and reliable arrow you can buy. Selecting the right arrows may be the single most important decision in archery and bowhunting.

General Principles

Though many hunters do not realize it, no arrow flies perfectly straight. When shot from a bow, an arrow bends dramatically and wobbles back and forth like a swimming trout. If this oscillation occurs at the right frequency, the arrow's path is relatively true; if not, the arrow flies poorly.

Manufacturers use the term *spine* to describe an arrow's stiffness, as determined by the amount the arrow bends when shot from a bow. When an archer has consistent difficulty making his arrows fly straight, it's usually because the arrow spine is mismatched for his bow.

The stiffness, or spine, of an arrow is governed by several variables, the most important of which are the diameter of the shaft, thickness of the outer walls, the length of the arrow and the weight of the head.

In general, the larger the diameter and thicker the walls of an arrow, the greater the spine. Manufacturers use a four-digit number to identify the diameter and wall thickness of an arrow (opposite page). In addition, the length of the shaft affects the arrow's

spring tension setting of an arrow rest can affect arrow flight enough to effectively change spine value. Even the release method can affect the bending of an arrow; arrows released with fingers bend somewhat more than those shot with a release aid.

Use the chart on the following page as a guide to selecting the right shafts when setting up any new bow and arrow combination. Or, if your current bow and arrow setup is not shooting to your satisfaction, consult the chart to make sure your shafts are spined correctly for the draw weight of your bow. These charts are updated as new arrows are developed and bow technology evolves. Check with your dealer at the time of purchase and confirm that you are using current data.

CONSISTENCY. Not only must arrow shafts be matched to a given bow, but they must be matched to each other. Small variations in length, diameter, head weight and fletching style can make it impossible to achieve consistent arrow flight. Your finished arrows should be identical in weight. Even with identical spine values, arrows with weight variations as small as 5 grains can have differing impact points at various ranges, especially with broadheads.

ARROW WEIGHT. As the spine chart shows, you have many choices of arrow weight within each given spine range. With increasing emphasis on speed, many archers choose the lightest shafts within the spine range. That's not a bad decision, but at some point the light-arrow game meets the law of diminishing returns, and you begin to lose more than you gain. Ultralight, high-speed arrows, particularly when equipped with broadheads, are more temperamental than heavier, slower arrows. Unless the shot is executed perfectly, very light arrows are likely to fly poorly. And, more seriously, light arrows increase the chances for bow damage. Heavy arrows absorb as much as 80 percent of a bow's energy, but lighter arrows absorb much less, leaving more energy to vibrate through the bow. If this vibration becomes excessive, as in the case of a dry fire (shooting a bow with no arrow on the string), a bow can break.

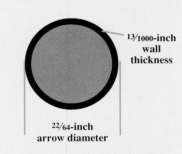

CROSS SECTION OF 2213 ARROW SHAFT

13/1000-inch wall thickness

22/64-inch arrow diameter

ALUMINUM ARROW SHAFTS are categorized with a four-digit number that identifies their diameter in 1/64-inch increments, and the thickness of the outer walls in 1/1000-inch increments. An arrow labeled 2213, for example, is 22/64 inch in diameter, and has walls 13/1000 inch thick.

also can affect spine, or at least change the way a shaft behaves when shot. A large fletching, for example, makes an arrow stiffer in flight. And the

spine; shorter shafts are stiffer than long shafts. For example, a 32-inch 2213 arrow will flex much more than a 26-inch 2213 arrow.

Finally, heavy arrowheads reduce an arrow's spine. That is, a 32-inch 2213 aluminum arrow with a 150-grain broadhead will flex more than an identical arrow equipped with a 100-grain head.

Other variables

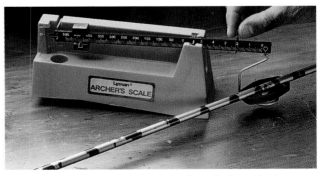

WEIGH arrows on an archer's or druggist's scale that measures in grains.

Hunting Shaft Size Selection Chart *(reprinted with permission from Easton arrows)*

COMPOUND BOW RELEASE AID
(Actual or calculated PEAK BOW WEIGHT-LBS.)

CORRECT ARROW LENGTH FOR HUNTING

NOTICE: FOR ARROW LENGTHS LONGER THAN 33": From your bow weight row, move down one row in the 33" column for each inch your arrow is longer than 33". FOR ARROW LENGTHS SHORTER THAN 23": From your bow weight row, move up one row in the 23" column

Round Wheel — Broadhead or Field Point Wt. only				Soft Cam — Broadhead or Field Point Wt. only				Hard Cam (Speed cam) — Broadhead or Field Point Wt. only				22½- **23"** -23½ (Size / Model / Weight)	23½- **24"** -24½ (Size / Model / Weight)	24½- **25"** -25½ (Size / Model / Weight)	25½- **26"** -26½ (Size / Model / Weight)
75 (65-85)	100 (90-110)	125 (115-135)	150 (140-160)	75 (65-85)	100 (90-110)	125 (115-135)	150 (140-160)	75 (65-85)	100 (90-110)	125 (115-135)	150 (140-160)				
50 to 55	47 to 52	44 to 49	41 to 46	45 to 50	42 to 47	39 to 44	36 to 41	40 to 45	37 to 42	34 to 39	31 to 36		1813 / 75 / 189 1716 / 75 / 217	**1913** / 75 / **209 A** **1816** / **75,E** / **232 B**	**1913** / 75 / **217 B** **1816** / **75,E** / 241 C
55 to 60	52 to 57	49 to 54	46 to 51	50 to 55	47 to 52	44 to 49	41 to 46	45 to 50	42 to 47	39 to 44	36 to 41	1813 / 75 / 181 1716 / 75 / 208	1913 / 75 / 200 A **1816** / **75,E** / **223 B**	**1913** / 75 / **209 B** **1816** / **75,E** / **232 C** 3L-18 5.4 / A/C/C P/C / 194 202	2013 / 75 / 234 A **1916** / **75,E** / 261 A
60 to 65	57 to 62	54 to 59	51 to 56	55 to 60	52 to 57	49 to 54	46 to 51	50 to 55	47 to 52	44 to 49	41 to 46	1913 / 75 / 192 A 1816 / 75,E / 213 B	**1913** / 75 / **200 B** **1816** / **75,E** / **223 C**	2013 / 75 / 225 A **1916** / **75,E** / **251 B** 3L-18 5.4 / A/C/C P/C / 186 194	**2013** / 75 / **234 B** **1916** / **75,E** / 261 B 3L-18 5.4 / A/C/C P/C / 194 202
65 to 70	62 to 67	59 to 64	56 to 61	60 to 65	57 to 62	54 to 59	51 to 56	55 to 60	52 to 57	49 to 54	46 to 51	**1913** / 75 / **192 B** **1816** / **75,E** / 213 C	2013 / 75 / 216 A **1916** / **75,E** / **241 B** 3L-18 5.4 / A/C/C P/C / 179 186	**2013** / 75 / **225 B** **1916** / **75,E** / **251 B** 3L-18 5.4 / A/C/C P/C / 186 194	2113 / 75 / 242 B 2016 / S,75 / 275 A 3-18 5.5 / A/C/C P/C / 203 214
70 to 76	67 to 73	64 to 70	61 to 67	65 to 70	62 to 67	59 to 64	56 to 61	60 to 65	57 to 62	54 to 59	51 to 56	2013 / 75 / 207 A 1916 / 75,E / 231 A 3L-18 5.4 / A/C/C P/C / 172 179	**2013** / **75** / **216 B** **1916** / **75,E** / **241 A** 3L-18 5.4 / A/C/C P/C / 179 186	2113 / 75 / 223 B 2016 / S,75 / 264 A 3-18 5.5 / A/C/C P/C / 195 206	2212 / S / 230 B **2114** / **S,75** / **256 B** 2016 / S,75 / 275 C 2115 / S,75 / 280 A **2018** / **S,75,E** / **319 A** 3-28 5.7 / A/C/C P/C / 211 229
76 to 82	73 to 79	70 to 76	67 to 73	70 to 76	67 to 73	64 to 70	61 to 67	65 to 70	62 to 67	59 to 64	56 to 61	**2013** / 75 / **207 B** **1916** / **75,E** / 231 B 3L-18 5.4 / A/C/C P/C / 172 179	2113 / 75 / 223 B 2016 / S,75 / 253 A 3-18 5.5 / A/C/C P/C / 187 197	2212 / S / 221 B **2114** / **S,75** / **247 B** 2016 / S,75 / 264 C 2115 / S,75 / 269 A **2018** / **S,75,E** / **307 A** 3-28 5.7 / A/C/C P/C / 203 221	2212 / S / 230 C **2113** / **S,75** / **256 A** 2114 / S,75 / 256 C 2115 / S,75 / 280 A **2018** / **S,75,E** / **319 B** 3-28 5.7 / A/C/C P/C / 211 229
82 to 88	79 to 85	76 to 82	73 to 79	76 to 82	73 to 79	70 to 76	67 to 73	70 to 76	67 to 73	64 to 70	61 to 67	2113 / 75 / 214 B 2016 / S,75 / 243 A 3-18 5.5 / A/C/C P/C / 180 189	2212 / S / 212 B **2114** / **S,75** / **237 B** 2016 / S,75 / 253 C 2115 / S,75 / 259 A **2018** / **S,75,E** / **295 A** 3-28 5.7 / A/C/C P/C / 194 212	2212 / S / 221 C **2113** / **S,75** / **246 A** 2114 / S,75 / 247 C 2115 / S,75 / 269 B **2018** / **S,75,E** / **307 B** 3-28 5.7 / A/C/C P/C / 203 221	2312 / S / 246 B 2213 / S,75 / 256 C **2215** / **S,75** / **277 B** 2117 / S,75,E / 313 A 3-39 5.9 / A/C/C P/C / 223 245
88 to 94	85 to 91	82 to 88	79 to 85	82 to 88	79 to 85	76 to 82	73 to 79	76 to 82	73 to 79	70 to 76	67 to 73	2212 / S / 203 B **2114** / **S,75** / **227 B** 2016 / S,75 / 243 C 2115 / S,75 / 248 A **2018** / **S,75,E** / **282 A** 3-28 5.7 / A/C/C P/C / 186 203	2212 / S / 212 C **2113** / **S,75** / **236 A** 2114 / S,75 / 237 C 2115 / S,75 / 259 B **2018** / **S,75,E** / **295 B** 3-28 5.7 / A/C/C P/C / 194 212	2312 / S / 237 B 2213 / S,75 / 246 C **2215** / **S,75** / **267 B** 2117 / S,75,E / 301 A 3-39 5.9 / A/C/C P/C / 215 235	2312 / S / 246 C **2314** / **S,75** / **277 A** 2215 / S,75 / 277 C 2117 / S,75,E / 313 B **2216** / **S** / **313 A** 3-49 6.1 / A/C/C P/C / 230 259
94 to 100	91 to 97	88 to 94	85 to 91	88 to 94	85 to 91	82 to 88	79 to 85	82 to 88	79 to 85	76 to 82	73 to 79	2212 / S / 203 C **2113** / **S,75** / **226 A** 2114 / S,75 / 227 C 2115 / S,75 / 248 B **2018** / **S,75,E** / **282 B** 3-28 5.7 / A/C/C P/C / 186 203	2312 / S / 228 B 2213 / S,75 / 236 C **2215** / **S,75** / **256 B** 2117 / S,75,E / 289 A 3-39 5.9 / A/C/C P/C / 206 206	2312 / S / 237 C **2314** / **S,75** / **266 A** 2215 / S,75 / 267 C 2117 / S,75,E / 301 B **2216** / **S** / **301 A** 3-49 6.1 / A/C/C P/C / 221 249	**2413** / **S,75** / **270 A** 2314 / S,75 / 277 B 2315 / S,75 / 303 A 2216 / S,75,E / 313 B 2219 / S,75,E / 358 A 3-49 6.1 / A/C/C P/C / 230 259
100 to 106	97 to 103	94 to 100	91 to 97	94 to 100	91 to 97	88 to 94	85 to 91	88 to 94	85 to 91	82 to 88	79 to 85	2312 / S / 218 B 2213 / S,75 / 226 C **2215** / **S,75** / **245 B** 2117 / S,75,E / 277 A 3-39 5.9 / A/C/C P/C / 197 216	2312 / S / 228 C **2314** / **S,75** / **255 A** 2215 / S,75 / 256 C 2117 / S,75,E / 289 B **2216** / **S** / **289 A** 3-49 6.1 / A/C/C P/C / 212 239	**2413** / **S,75** / **260 A** 2314 / S,75 / 266 B 2315 / S,75 / 292 A 2216 / S,75,E / 301 B 2219 / S,75,E / 344 A 3-49 6.1 / A/C/C P/C / 221 249	2512 / S / 267 A 2413 / S,75 / 270 B **2315** / **S,75** / **303 B** 2219 / S,75,E / 358 B 3-60 6.3 / A/C/C P/C / 246 274
106 to 112	103 to 109	100 to 106	97 to 103	100 to 106	97 to 103	94 to 100	91 to 97	94 to 100	91 to 97	88 to 94	85 to 91	2312 / S / 218 C **2314** / **S,75** / **244 A** 2215 / S,75 / 245 C 2117 / S,75,E / 277 B **2216** / **S,75** / **277 A** 3-49 6.1 / A/C/C P/C / 203 229	**2413** / **S,75** / **250 A** 2314 / S,75 / 255 B **2315** / **S,75** / **280 A** 2216 / S,75 / 289 B 2219 / S,75,E / 329 A 3-49 6.1 / A/C/C P/C / 212 239	2512 / S / 257 A 2413 / S,75 / 260 B **2315** / **S,75** / **292 B** 2219 / S,75,E / 344 B 3-60 6.3 / A/C/C P/C / 236 264	2512 / S / 267 A 2315 / S,75 / 303 B 2219 / S,75,E / 358 B 3-60 6.3 / A/C/C P/C / 246 274

- This chart was set up using: • Recurve bows with finger release • High-performance, 50-65% let-off compound bows with release aids • Fast Flight strings.
- The chart indicates that more than one shaft size may shoot well from your bow. **Shaft sizes in bold type are the most widely used aluminum sizes,** but you may decide to shoot a lighter shaft for speed or a heavier shaft for greater durability and penetration. Also, large variations in bow efficiency, type of wheels or cams, bow length, string material, and type of release may require special bow tuning or a shaft size change to accommodate these variations.
- **"Shaft Weight"** column–indicates bare shaft weight only. To determine the total arrow weight, add the weights of the shaft, point, insert, nock and fletching. Where two aluminum shaft models are shown for one size, the weight listed is for XX75. Letter codes A-C listed to the right of the shaft weight indicate the relative stiffness of each aluminum shaft within that "Shaft Size" box ("A" being the stiffest, "B" less stiff, etc.).

ALUMINUM SHAFT CHART allows you to pick appropriate shafts. 1) Determine the weight of your broadhead or field point. 2) Choose the column that best describes your bow; use the left side if you shoot a compound bow and use a release aid; use the right side if you shoot a recurve. 3) Choose the *Head Weight Only* column that matches the weight of your

CORRECT ARROW LENGTH FOR HUNTING

for each inch your arrow is shorter than 23". FOR BOW WEIGHTS HEAVIER THAN INDICATED ON THE CHART: From your arrow length column, move to the right one column (1" longer shaft) for each 6 lbs. your bow is heavier than the maximum weights shown. FOR COMPOUND BOWS WITH FINGER RELEASE: From your bow weight row, move one row heavier (one row down).

RECURVE BOW FINGER RELEASE

Actual or calculated PEAK BOW WEIGHT-LBS.

26½- 27" -27½			27½- 28" -28½			28½- 29" -29½			29½- 30" -30½			30½- 31" -31½			31½- 32" -32½			32½- 33" -33½			Broadhead or Field Point Wt. only			
Shaft Size	Shaft Model	Shaft Weight	Shaft Size	Shaft Model	Shaft Weight	Shaft Size	Shaft Model	Shaft Weight	Shaft Size	Shaft Model	Shaft Weight	Shaft Size	Shaft Model	Shaft Weight	Shaft Size	Shaft Model	Shaft Weight	Shaft Size	Shaft Model	Shaft Weight	75 (grains) 65-85	100 (grains) 90-110	125 (grains) 115-135	150 (grains) 140-160
2013 **1916** 3L-18 5.4	75 **75,E** A/C/C P/C	243 A **271 A** 201 210	**2013** **1916** 3L-18 5.4	**75** **75,E** A/C/C P/C	**252 B** **281 B** 209 218	2113 **2016** 3-18 5.5	75 **S,75** A/C/C P/C	270 B **306 A** 226 238	2212 **2114** 2016 2115 **2018** 3-28 5.7	S **S,75** S,75 S,75 **S,75,E** A/C/C P/C	265 B **296 B** 317 C 323 A **368 A** 243 265	2212 **2113** 2114 2115 **2018** 3-28 5.7	S **S,75** S,75 S,75 **S,75,E** A/C/C P/C	274 C **305 A** 306 C 334 B **381 B** 251 273	2312 2213 **2215** **2117** 3-39 5.9	S S,75 **S,75** **S,75,E** A/C/C P/C	303 B 315 C **341 B** **385 A** 275 301	2312 **2314** 2215 2117 **2216** 3-49 6.1	S **S,75** S,75 S,75,E **S,75** A/C/C P/C	313 C **351 A** 352 C 397 B **397 A** 291	35 to 40	32 to 37	29 to 34	26 to 31
2013 **1916** 3L-18 5.4	**75** **75,E** A/C/C P/C	**243 B** **271 B** 201 210	2113 **2016** 3-18 5.5	75 **S,75** A/C/C P/C	260 B **296 A** 219 230	2212 **2114** 2016 2115 **2018** 3-28 5.7	S **S,75** S,75 S,75 **S,75,E** A/C/C P/C	256 B **286 B** 306 C 312 A **356 A** 235 256	2212 **2113** 2114 2115 **2018** 3-28 5.7	S **S,75** S,75 S,75 **S,75,E** A/C/C P/C	265 C **295 A** 296 C 323 B **368 B** 243 265	2312 2213 **2215** **2117** 3-39 5.9	S S,75 **S,75** **S,75,E** A/C/C P/C	294 B 305 C **331 B** **373 A** 266 292	2312 **2314** 2215 2117 **2216** 3-49 6.1	S **S,75** S,75 S,75,E **S,75** A/C/C P/C	303 C **341 A** 341 C 385 B **385 A** 283 318	**2413** 2314 **2315** 2216 2219 3-49 6.1	**S,75** S,75 **S,75** S,75 S,75,E A/C/C P/C	**343 A** 351 B **385 A** 397 B 454 A 291	40 to 45	37 to 42	34 to 39	31 to 36
2113 **2016** 3-18 5.5	75 **S,75** A/C/C P/C	251 B **285 A** 211 222	2212 **2114** 2016 2115 **2018** 3-28 5.7	S **S,75** S,75 S,75 **S,75,E** A/C/C P/C	248 B **276 B** 296 C 302 A **344 A** 227 247	2212 **2113** 2114 2115 **2018** 3-28 5.7	S **S,75** S,75 S,75 **S,75,E** A/C/C P/C	256 C **285 A** 286 C 312 B **356 B** 235 256	2312 2213 **2215** **2117** 3-39 5.9	S S,75 **S,75** **S,75,E** A/C/C P/C	284 B 295 C **320 B** **361 A** 257 282	2312 **2314** 2215 2117 **2216** 3-49 6.1	S **S,75** S,75 S,75,E **S,75** A/C/C P/C	294 C **330 A** 331 C 373 B **373 A** 274 308	**2413** 2314 **2315** 2216 2219 3-49 6.1	**S,75** S,75 **S,75** S,75 S,75,E A/C/C P/C	**333 A** 341 B **373 A** 385 B 441 A 283 318	2512 2413 **2315** **2219** 3-60 6.3	S S,75 **S,75** **S,75,E** A/C/C P/C	339 A 343 B **385 B** **454 B** 312 348	45 to 50	42 to 47	39 to 44	36 to 41
2212 **2114** 2016 2115 **2018** 3-28 5.7	S **S,75** S,75 S,75 **S,75,E** A/C/C P/C	239 B **266 B** 285 C 291 A **332 A** 219 238	2212 **2113** 2114 2115 **2018** 3-28 5.7	S **S,75** S,75 S,75 **S,75,E** A/C/C P/C	248 C **275 A** 276 C 302 B **344 B** 227 247	2312 2213 **2215** **2117** 3-39 5.9	S S,75 **S,75** **S,75,E** A/C/C P/C	275 B 285 C **309 B** **349 A** 249 273	2312 **2314** 2215 2117 **2216** 3-49 6.1	S **S,75** S,75 S,75,E **S,75** A/C/C P/C	284 C **319 A** 320 C 361 B **361 A** 265 299	**2413** 2314 **2315** 2216 2219 3-49 6.1	**S,75** S,75 **S,75** S,75 S,75,E A/C/C P/C	**322 A** 330 B **362 A** 373 B 427 A 274 308	2512 2413 **2315** **2219** 3-60 6.3	S S,75 **S,75** **S,75,E** A/C/C P/C	329 A 333 B **373 B** **441 B** 302 338	2512 **2315** 2219 3-60 6.3	S **S,75** S,75,E A/C/C P/C	339 A **385 B** 454 B 312 348	50 to 55	47 to 52	44 to 49	41 to 46
2212 **2113** 2114 2115 **2018** 3-28 5.7	S **S,75** S,75 S,75 **S,75,E** A/C/C P/C	239 C **265 A** 266 C 291 B **332 B** 219 238	2312 2213 **2215** **2117** 3-39 5.9	S S,75 **S,75** **S,75,E** A/C/C P/C	265 B 275 C **299 B** **337 A** 240 263	2312 **2314** 2215 2117 **2216** 3-49 6.1	S **S,75** S,75 S,75,E **S,75** A/C/C P/C	275 C **309 A** 309 C 349 B **349 A** 256 289	**2413** 2314 **2315** 2216 2219 3-49 6.1	**S,75** S,75 **S,75** S,75 S,75,E A/C/C P/C	**312 A** 319 B **350 A** 361 B 413 A 265 299	2512 2413 **2315** **2219** 3-60 6.3	S S,75 **S,75** **S,75,E** A/C/C P/C	318 A 322 B **362 B** **427 B** 293 327	2512 **2315** 2219 3-60 6.3	S **S,75** S,75,E A/C/C P/C	329 A **373 B** 441 B 302 338	2512 **2514** **2317** 3-71 6.5	S **S,75** **S,75** A/C/C P/C	339 B **374 A** **438 A** 327 374	55 to 60	52 to 57	49 to 54	46 to 51
2312 2213 **2215** **2117** 3-39 5.9	S S,75 **S,75** **S,75,E** A/C/C P/C	256 B 265 C **288 B** **325 A** 232 254	2312 **2314** 2215 2117 **2216** 3-49 6.1	S **S,75** S,75 S,75,E **S,75** A/C/C P/C	265 C **298 A** 299 C 337 B **337 A** 247 279	**2413** 2314 **2315** 2216 2219 3-49 6.1	**S,75** S,75 **S,75** S,75 S,75,E A/C/C P/C	**302 A** 309 B **338 A** 349 B 399 A 256 289	2512 2413 **2315** **2219** 3-60 6.3	S S,75 **S,75** **S,75,E** A/C/C P/C	308 A 312 B **350 B** **413 B** 284 317	2512 **2315** 2219 3-60 6.3	S **S,75** S,75,E A/C/C P/C	318 A **362 B** 427 B 293 327	2512 **2514** **2317** 3-71 6.5	S **S,75** **S,75** A/C/C P/C	329 B **363 A** **424 A** 317 363	**2514** 2613 **2317** 2419 3-71 6.5	**S,75** S **S,75** 75 A/C/C P/C	**374 B** 379 A **438 B** 480 A 327 374	60 to 65	57 to 62	54 to 59	51 to 56
2312 **2314** 2215 2117 **2216** 3-49 6.1	S **S,75** S,75 S,75,E **S,75** A/C/C P/C	256 C **287 A** 288 C 325 B **325 A** 238 269	**2413** 2314 **2315** 2216 2219 3-49 6.1	**S,75** S,75 **S,75** S,75 S,75,E A/C/C P/C	**291 A** 298 B **327 A** 337 B 386 A 247 279	2512 2413 **2315** **2219** 3-60 6.3	S S,75 **S,75** **S,75,E** A/C/C P/C	298 A 302 B **338 B** **399 B** 274 306	2512 **2315** 2219 3-60 6.3	S **S,75** S,75,E A/C/C P/C	308 A **350 B** 413 B 284 317	2512 **2514** **2317** 3-71 6.5	S **S,75** **S,75** A/C/C P/C	318 B **351 A** **411 A** 308 352	**2514** 2613 **2317** 2419 3-71 6.5	**S,75** S **S,75** 75 A/C/C P/C	**363 B** 368 A **424 B** 466 A 317 363	2514 2613 2317 **2419** 3-71 6.5	S,75 S S,75 **75** A/C/C P/C	374 B 379 A 438 B **480 A** 327 374	65 to 70	62 to 67	59 to 64	56 to 61
2413 2314 **2315** 2216 2219 3-49 6.1	**S,75** S,75 **S,75** S,75 S,75,E A/C/C P/C	**281 A** 287 B **315 A** 325 B 372 A 238 269	2512 2413 **2315** **2219** 3-60 6.3	S S,75 **S,75** **S,75,E** A/C/C P/C	288 A 291 B **327 B** **386 B** 265 295	2512 **2315** 2219 3-60 6.3	S **S,75** S,75,E A/C/C P/C	298 A **338 B** 399 B 274 306	2512 **2514** **2317** 3-71 6.5	S **S,75** **S,75** A/C/C P/C	308 B **340 A** **398 A** 298 340	**2514** 2613 **2317** 2419 3-71 6.5	**S,75** S **S,75** 75 A/C/C P/C	**351 B** 356 A **411 B** 451 A 308 352	2514 2613 2317 **2419** 3-71 6.5	S,75 S S,75 **75** A/C/C P/C	363 B 368 A 424 B **466 A** 317 363	2613 2419	S 75	379 A 480 B	70 to 76	67 to 73	64 to 70	61 to 67
2512 2413 **2315** **2219** 3-60 6.3	S S,75 **S,75** **S,75,E** A/C/C P/C	277 A 281 B **315 B** **372 B** 255 285	2512 **2315** 2219 3-60 6.3	S **S,75** S,75,E A/C/C P/C	288 A **327 B** 386 B 265 295	2512 **2514** **2317** 3-71 6.5	S **S,75** **S,75** A/C/C P/C	298 B **329 A** **385 A** 288 329	**2514** 2613 **2317** 2419 3-71 6.5	**S,75** S **S,75** 75 A/C/C P/C	**340 B** 345 A **398 B** 437 A 298 340	2514 2613 2317 **2419** 3-71 6.5	S,75 S S,75 **75** A/C/C P/C	351 B 356 A 411 B **451 A** 308 352	2613 2419	S 75	368 A 466 B	2613	S	379	76 to 82	73 to 79	70 to 76	67 to 73
2512 **2315** 2219 3-60 6.3	S **S,75** S,75,E A/C/C P/C	277 A **315 B** 372 B 255 285	2512 **2514** **2317** 3-71 6.5	S **S,75** **S,75** A/C/C P/C	288 B **317 A** **371 A** 278 318	**2514** 2613 **2317** 2419 3-71 6.5	**S,75** S **S,75** 75 A/C/C P/C	**329 B** 333 A **385 B** 422 A 288 329	2514 2613 2317 **2419** 3-71 6.5	S,75 S S,75 **75** A/C/C P/C	340 B 345 A 398 B **437 A** 298 340	2613 2419	S 75	356 A 451 B	2613	S	368				82 to 88	79 to 85	76 to 82	73 to 79
2512 **2514** **2317** 3-71 6.5	S **S,75** **S,75** A/C/C P/C	277 B **306 A** **358 A** 268 306	**2514** 2613 **2317** 2419 3-71 6.5	**S,75** S **S,75** 75 A/C/C P/C	**317 B** 322 A **371 B** 407 A 278 318	2514 2613 2317 **2419** 3-71 6.5	S,75 S S,75 **75** A/C/C P/C	329 B 333 A 385 B **422 A** 288 329	2613 2419	S 75	345 A 437 A	2613	S	356							88 to 94	85 to 91	82 to 88	79 to 85

WARNING: Over-stressing compound bows by using arrows lighter than AMO recommendations may cause damage to the bow and possible injury to the shooter.

AMO compound bow manufacturers have issued the following warning:

- Total arrow weight (shaft weight [shown on Easton chart] plus weight of point, insert [if used] and fletching plus nock) should be greater than 6 grains per pound of peak bow weight for a 60# compound bow with a 30" draw length.
- Bow weights lighter than 60# and draw lengths shorter than 30" can use arrows lighter than 6 grains/pound of peak bow weight.
- Bow weights heavier than 60# and draw lengths longer than 30" should use arrows heavier than 6 grains/pound of peak bow weight.

"Shaft Size" column—indicates suggested shaft sizes.
"Shaft Model"— designates arrow model.
"S" = XX78® Super Slam® shafts. Also XX78 Camo Extreme™ Predator® shafts in sizes 2213, 2314,2413, and 2514. Size 2613 is available in Camo Extreme only (7178 alloy).
"75" = XX75®, Autumn Orange®, Easton Classic®, Camo Hunter®, Advantage™, Gamegetter® II, and Gamegetter® (7075 alloy).

"E" = Eagle® shafts (5086 alloy).
"A/C/C®" = Aluminum/Carbon/Competition shafts.
"P/C®" = Pure/Carbon shafts.
Bowhunting with A/C/C and P/C: Carbon (graphite) arrows may be used for hunting if special precautions are taken. See dealer or the Easton information packed with A/C/C, P/C or Specter shafts.

broadheads or field points, then move down the column to the box that matches your peak bow weight. 4) Move horizontally across the row to the column listing your *Correct Arrow Length*. 5) Select an arrow size from one of those listed at the intersection of the bow weight and correct arrow length. The most widely used sizes are listed in boldface.

AMO Minimum Recommended Arrow Weights
S.E.= stored energy, E.S.E.= energy storage efficiency, B.H.= brace height, P.D.F.= peak draw force

Actual Peak Bow Weight (lbs.)				Minimum Recommended Arrow Weights (grains)								
RECURVE	ROUND WHEEL	SOFT CAM (Energy Wheel)	HARD CAM (Speed Cam)	AMO DRAW LENGTH (in)								
$\frac{S.E.^{**}}{P.D.F.}$ = .95 E.S.E. 62 B.H. 9.5	$\frac{S.E.^{**}}{P.D.F.}$ = 1.04 E.S.E. 75.1 B.H. 7.0	$\frac{S.E.^{**}}{P.D.F.}$ = 1.20 E.S.E. 71.3 B.H. 8.0	$\frac{S.E.^{**}}{P.D.F.}$ = 1.3+ E.S.E. 65.6 B.H. 9.0	25	26	27	28	29	30	31	32	33
33	32	29	27	150	150	150	150	150	150	150	150	150
34-41	33-38	30-35	28-32	150	150	150	150	150	150	150	151	165
42-46	39-43	36-39	33-36	150	150	150	150	150	163	179	195	211
47-52	44-49	40-44	37-41	150	150	150	167	185	203	222	240	258
53-58	50-54	45-49	42-46	150	163	183	203	224	244	264	285	305
59-63	55-60	50-54	47-50	172	195	217	240	262	284	307	329	352
64-69	61-64	55-59	51-55	202	227	251	276	300	325	350	374	339
70-75	65-71	60-64	56-60	232	259	286	312	339	365	392	419	445
76-81	72-76	65-70	61-65	262	291	320	348	377	406	435	463	492
82-86	77-81	71-74	66-69	292	323	354	385	416	446	477	508	539
87-92	82-87	75-79	70-74	322	355	388	421	454	487	520	553	586
93-99	88-94	80-85	75-80	352	387	422	457	492	532	581	629	676

AMO Draw Length = A + 1 ¾"

Pivot point to bottom of nock groove = A

Riser

1 ¾"

**STORED ENERGY based on: •360-grain arrow, •30" draw length, •60-lb. peak weight, •speed (hard) cam.
*ARROW WEIGHTS are measured in grains and include all arrow components – shaft, insert, point, fletching and nock.

USING THE "AMO MINIMUM RECOMMENDED ARROW WEIGHT" CHART: (1) Choose the column on the left that best describes the bow you shoot. (2) Move down this column until you find the weight range of your bow's peak bow weight. (3) Move right across the row until you reach the column that matches your bow's draw length. This entry gives the minimum recommended arrow weight for your bow.

The old standard rule of thumb recommended 9 grains of arrow weight for every pound of draw weight. For a 60-pound bow, that translates to 540-grain arrows (9 grains × 60 pounds draw weight = 540-grain arrows).

The old formula is antiquated, given modern bow and arrow construction, but the principle of using draw weight to determine arrow weight still applies. Some manufacturers recommend 6 grains of arrow weight per pound of draw weight – a good all-around guideline. The formula has been refined even further by the AMO (Archery Manufacturers and Merchants Association). The accompanying chart (opposite page) shows the AMO's recommendations, which take into account not only draw weight, but wheel design and draw length, as well. Following this chart ensures a safe and reasonably efficient bow and arrow combination. Pushing to the extremes beyond this chart could yield explosive – and unpleasant – results.

Shaft Materials

ALUMINUM. Arrow shafts made from aluminum have been the standard for years, and remain so today, for several reasons. Aluminum arrows are remarkably consistent in size and weight, thanks to precise manufacturing processes. The shafts are formed by pulling aluminum tubes across a mandrel until they meet exact specifications for diameter,

Straightening Bent Arrows

S traightening arrows takes time and practice but is not difficult to learn. Over time, this process can save the bowhunter a lot of arrows and money.

First, adjust the rollers (A, B) so they are evenly spaced from the indicator (C) and cover the length of the bend in the arrow. Place the bent arrow on the rollers, then adjust the indicator so the tip of it remains in contact with the arrow at all times when you rotate the shaft on the rollers. Now, using an arrow you know is straight, adjust the dial on the indicator to zero. Next, place the bent arrow back on the rollers and rotate the shaft gently with a finger placed over a roller, until the point with the greatest bend is facing up. Depress the lever (D) to straighten the shaft. Aluminum arrows rebound slightly, so press down until the indicator goes past zero. Finally, check the entire length of shaft for straightness.

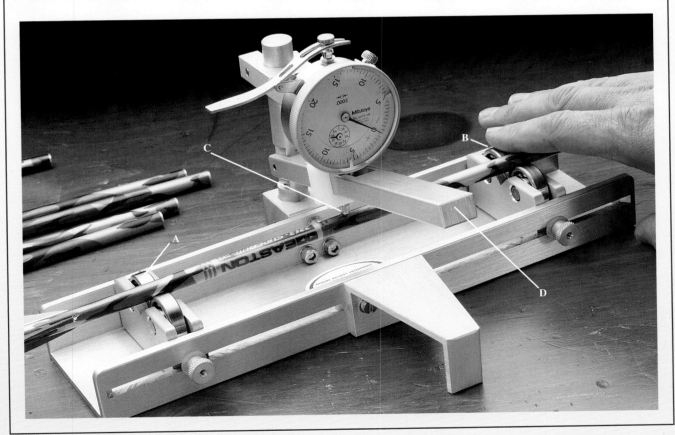

ARROW SHAFT MATERIALS include: (A) wood, (B) aluminum, (C) aluminum-carbon (inset) and (D) carbon.

wall thickness and weight. The shafts are then straightened by machine to tolerances as fine as .0015 inch.

Aluminum shafts are available in more than 50 sizes, with diameters ranging from 14/64 to 26/64 inch, and wall thicknesses from .011 to .019 inch. With this broad range, archers can choose just the right combination of spine and weight for a given bow and hunting situation, from ultralight for greatest speed to ultraheavy for durability and maximum energy.

Although thin-walled shafts can bend and break, aluminum arrows with thick walls will hold up well under tough hunting conditions. And aluminum shafts can be straightened and reused, making them a good value.

Another convenient feature of aluminum shafts is the use of head and nock inserts made of aluminum or carbon. Aluminum inserts are anchored with hot-melt glue (right). Carbon inserts, which weigh 10 to 15 grains less than aluminum, depending on arrow size, are generally installed with epoxy. Aluminum nock inserts allow you to remove and rotate the head and nock simply by heating the glue.

Aluminum arrows come in a multitude of camouflage designs and colors to fit every situation – and to please every archer. Finally, aluminum arrows are available to fit every budget, from the economical Gamegetters® to the very popular XX75® and durable XX78®.

CARBON. Several companies make all-carbon or carbon-composite arrow shafts. These shafts are characterized by their small diameter and by their light weight. Even at maximum length and stiffness, carbon shafts are relatively light. This provides an obvious speed advantage for the hunter who seeks fast arrows but wants to keep the kinetic energy.

Carbon shafts do not stay bent, so you'll never need to straighten them, but they can break when they hit a hard object, sometimes explosively. Probably the biggest threat to carbon is a side blow from another arrow; a shaft that is chipped or creased is unusable. Unlike aluminum shafts, which can be straightened, damaged carbon arrows must be discarded.

Most arrow penetration tests into Styrofoam® or Ethafoam® give carbon arrows the edge over aluminum arrows with comparable spine, due mostly to the smaller diameter. The small-diameter shaft drifts slightly less in a strong crosswind. Many hunters also believe that the narrower carbon shafts penetrate better than aluminum on animals, though some experts dispute this position, arguing that the hole made by a broadhead is so much larger than the shaft diameter that penetration is unlikely to be affected.

One potential problem with the small diameter of carbon arrows is inadequate rest clearance, especially when a shoot-through rest is used. With a large-diameter aluminum shaft, the support arms of the rest can be spread far apart, giving plenty of room for the fletching to clear. But with carbon shafts, the support arms must be placed close together to cradle the narrow arrow, and the fletching must be lined up perfectly to slip between the arms (below).

Traditionally, carbon shafts were too small in diameter to accept inserts like those used with aluminum shafts. As a result, heads were attached with adapters

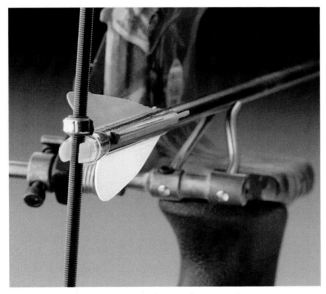

Arms of your arrow rest must be set close together to support narrow carbon arrows, and the fletching must be aligned perfectly

called *outserts*, which slipped over the end of the shafts. That system was replaced by one or two piece inserts, which helped with consistent arrow flight and ease of changing heads.

Originally, carbon arrows seemed designed strictly for compound bow shooters seeking speed, but in recent years some recurve and longbow shooters also have switched to carbon arrows. One reason is the stiff spine in relation to weight. Many traditional archers prefer wood shafts, but a stick bow shooter with a long draw length often has difficulty buying adequately spined wood shafts. With carbon, he can get plenty of spine at virtually any arrow length. A second reason is the small diameter of carbon arrows. Unlike compound bows, many recurves and longbows

are not cut past center. This makes carbon attractive, because the small-diameter shaft rests closer to the center of the bow than does a large diameter wood or aluminum shaft.

Although early carbon arrows were prohibitively expensive, the development of new grades of carbon and carbon-composites has put lower-end carbon shafts in a price range comparable to many aluminum shafts.

Though not traditionally available for hunters using carbon arrows, camouflage patterns are now available from most manufacturers.

ALUMINUM/CARBON. Gaining in popularity is the A/C/C shaft (Aluminum/Carbon/Competition), which consists of a small-diameter aluminum core encased in three layers of carbon fibers. These shafts combine the best attributes of both aluminum and carbon. With the aluminum core, A/C arrows can be manufactured to the same precise straightness tolerances as the finest grade aluminum arrows. And with the carbon overlay, A/C arrows can be smaller in diameter and lighter in weight without compromising stiffness. For a given spine value, A/C shafts are the lightest available. This, along with their precision straightness, makes them favored shafts among professional 3-D shooters.

Most A/C shafts are slightly larger in diameter than all-carbon shafts, and, with the aluminum core, they will accept standard, flush-fitting nock and head adapters.

A/C shafts are very durable, but, like carbon shafts, they may break when striking a rock or other immovable objects. The main concern is a side blow. A glancing blow that skins off even one layer of carbon can drastically change the spine value of the shaft. If A/C arrows slap together in a target or glance off a hard object, you must check them carefully for damage.

WOOD. At one time, cedar shafts were the only game in town, and cedar arrows still have a strong following among ardent stick bow shooters. Some archers believe wood is superior because it has flexing qualities that make arrows more forgiving. Most archers agree that wood arrows do not perform as consistently as aluminum or carbon.

Because wood varies greatly in density and weight, cedar shafts must be methodically matched for spine and weight, a time-consuming process that adds to their cost. Well-matched cedar shafts are accurate, and they're beautiful – virtual works of art. But they also cost just as much as – or more than – other shaft materials.

Wood shafts also leave something to be desired in terms of durability because they break fairly easily and can warp in wet weather.

NOCKS include: (1) two-piece inserts for any type of shaft material and (2) one-piece nocks, which are glued directly to a swaged shaft.

Nocks

The nock on an arrow is little more than a tiny piece of plastic, yet it is critical to arrow performance. A nock should snap snugly onto the string, but should not be so tight that it hinders the arrow during release. Release-aid shooters generally want nocks a little tighter than finger shooters, to prevent arrows from falling off the string. Consistency is crucial; all arrows should fit the string identically. Once you find a nock that fits your bowstring perfectly, use the same brand and size on all your arrows.

It is even more critical that nocks are straight. A crooked nock pushes an arrow sideways from the instant you release the string, causing it to fly erratically. If, when shooting arrow groups in practice, one arrow consistently hits out of the group, check the nock for straightness by holding the arrow loose-

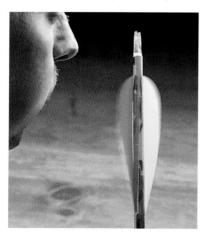

ly and blowing on the fletching to spin the arrow (left). If you see any wobble in the nock, replace it. Several companies make arrow spinners to check nock and head straightness. This simple operation can significantly improve your accuracy.

Fletching

Fletching, the group of fins attached to the back of an arrow, is what guides an arrow on a straight path in flight. Fletching can be made from plastic or from feathers – usually the primary wing feathers from a turkey.

FEATHERS OR PLASTIC?
Many hunters debate the value of feathers versus plastic vanes. Some arguments are subjective, based on personal preference, but others are objective. As a rule, vanes are more durable than feathers. Made from urethane, vinyl or Mylar®, vanes can withstand thousands of practice shots. Even smashed in a bow case, good urethane vanes will spring back to their original shape. Smooth and flexible, plastic vanes also are quieter than feathers, which can make aggravating noise when raked against brush.

Though feathers quickly become worn and tattered, they are more forgiving than vanes, especially for traditional archers shooting recurves or longbows. If you shoot off the shelf, as most traditional archers do, then feathers are the only choice. Feathers compress and slide past the shelf smoothly, while vanes bounce off the shelf, causing the arrow to fly every which way.

Feathers

On compound bows, which have specialized arrow rests and cutout risers, fletching clearance is rarely a problem. Nevertheless, some top-flight shooters still prefer feathers. Feathers are lighter, giving greater initial arrow speed, and they can be more stable, especially with broadheads. Some professional archers, including Randy Ulmer and Dave Holt, argue that they score consistently tighter broadhead groups with feathers than with vanes. Some archers, of course, prefer feathers for the same reasons they shoot cedar shafts – tradition.

FLETCHING SIZE. No exact formula can prescribe the correct fletching size. In general, the bigger the

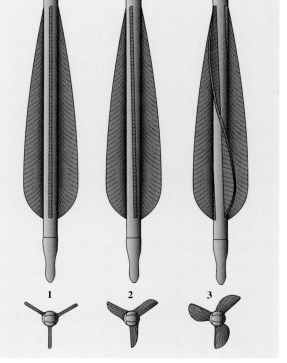

ATTACHMENT OF FLETCHES can be (1) straight, (2) offset or (3) helical.

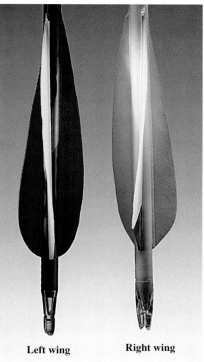

Left wing   **Right wing**

FEATHERS are wrapped left if they are left-wing feathers (left), or right if they are right-wing feathers (right).

broadhead, the bigger the fletching needed to control the arrow. Over the years, three 5-inch vanes or feathers have become the standard for controlling average-size broadheads. But with the trend toward lighter arrows, more hunters are turning to three 4-inch fletches to reduce weight. This configuration is ample when shooting precision-made broadheads no more than 1¼ inches wide.

Plastic vane

Some hunters prefer four fletches over three, believing that the greater surface area gives better arrow control. Four fletches allow the shooter to nock an arrow either way without fear of getting the cock

4-fletch arrow

feather or vane in the wrong direction. Three fletches, however, give better rest clearance, since they are farther apart on the shaft.

Much the way rifling in a gun barrel spins a bullet, the fletching must cause an arrow to rotate in flight. To provide this rotation on aluminum arrows, the fletches are attached at a slight angle on the shaft. Some hunters insist on strong helical fletching that wraps around the shaft, but this is not necessary unless you're shooting outsized broadheads. Mild helical fletching, which twists the vanes slightly around the shaft, is enough to stabilize average-size broadheads on a well-tuned bow.

On carbon arrows, however, a helical attachment is impossible, since the shafts are too small in diameter to wrap the fletches. In addition, a straight fletch clears the rest better. On carbon arrows, the fletching is attached with an offset of only 1 to 2 degrees.

Does it matter whether you twist or offset the fletching to the right or left? Vanes have no grain, so it makes no difference. Getting clearance past the rest is most important, so use whichever twist best clears the rest. With feathers, the direction of twist depends on whether the feathers are from the right wing or left wing of the bird: left-wing feathers must be twisted to the left; right-wing feathers, to the right. But it makes no difference whether you choose right or left feathers: a right-handed archer can shoot left-wing feathers, and vice versa.

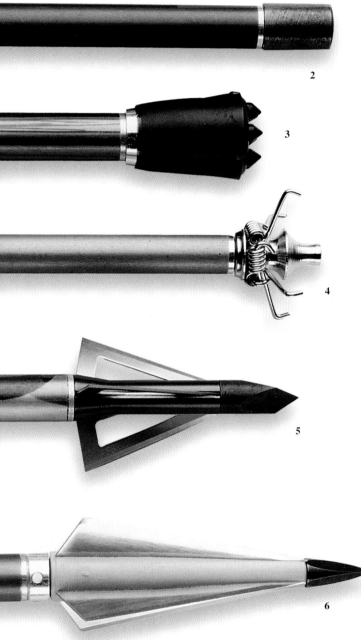

CHOOSING the proper heads for your arrows depends on their purpose and your personal preferences. Arrowheads include: (1) field point, (2) steel blunt, (3) rubber blunt, (4) judo point, (5) three-blade broadhead and (6) four-blade broadhead.

Heads

Arrowheads come in many styles to meet different needs, from rubber blunts for target shooting to oversize, four-blade broadheads for hunting the largest game animals. Broadheads used for hunting game must have two virtues: they must allow the arrow to fly true, and they must cut and penetrate when they reach the target.

GENERAL-PURPOSE HEADS. Field points, available in weights from 65 grains up to 180 grains, are standard for practice, as well as for target and 3-D shooting. These come in various diameters to match different shaft sizes.

For stump-shooting and other field practice, steel or rubber blunts work well. Practice heads with spring arms, like the Zwickey JUDO® point, may be even better in tall grass and leaves, because the spring arms prevent arrows from skipping long distances or sliding out of sight under cover.

For small game, including grouse, rabbits and squirrels, rubber blunts deliver a lot of shocking power and kill cleanly. Don't shoot small game with field points or steel blunts; the arrows simply pass through the animals, but do not kill them quickly and cleanly.

BROADHEADS. The most popular broadheads in recent years have been three-blade, replaceable-blade heads in 125- and 100-grain weights, with a cutting diameter of $1\frac{1}{8}$ to $1\frac{1}{4}$ inches. Experienced bowhunters have found that three-blade heads give optimum cutting surface and penetration, and fly true with little planing. Heads of that design and size are a good starting point for any new bowhunter.

Increasing surface area by adding a fourth blade or increasing overall length and width of the broadhead increases the potential for planing and requires special fletching. To control an arrow with oversized broadheads, the fletches must either be larger or radically helical. Oversized broadheads belong only on heavy arrows with lots of fletching.

At the other extreme, hunters shooting extremely light, fast arrows often change to low-profile broadheads with a diameter of 1 inch or less to achieve optimum arrow flight. These heads are very accurate, but obviously have a reduced cutting diameter, which could be a drawback.

Regardless of broadhead size, precision is key for best flight. A broadhead acts as a wing on the front of an arrow, and if that wing is crooked, the arrow will fly erratically. To check a broadhead for straightness, install it on an arrow, stand the arrow on the broadhead's tip, and spin it (below). Try different brands of broadheads until you find one that's consistently straight. If you find an occasional out-of-line head, you can straighten it on a precision arrow straightener.

Durability is also important when choosing broadheads. If a broadhead bends or breaks upon impact with an animal, it obviously won't achieve good penetration. Before shooting any brand of broadheads on game, test a few by shooting them into a durable foam 3-D target (below).

Balance is critical if an arrow is to fly well. Most experienced bowhunters recommend that arrows be balanced 10 to 12 percent forward of the center (FOC).

Expandable Broadheads

The expandable (open-on-impact) head is a specialty broadhead that has a strong following. In flight, the blades remain folded into the head; upon impact, the blades fold out for conventional broadhead performance. In theory, expandable broadheads offer the accuracy of field points and a cutting diameter wider than most fixed-blade broadheads.

Expandable broadheads have received mixed reviews, especially when used with light-poundage bows. For best results, test various brands of expanding broadheads on 3-D targets before using them on game. When hunting, wait for good broadside shots to avoid deflection problems. And shoot plenty of draw weight to ensure adequate penetration.

Tips for Broadheads

CHECK a broadhead for straightness by spinning the arrow on its tip. As it spins, watch the point at which the head and arrow meet. If you see any wobble, the broadhead is not straight – and probably will not fly true.

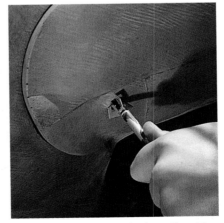

TEST the durability of a broadhead by shooting it into a foam 3-D target. If the head comes apart or bends after shooting it into the target, don't use it for game. Try another style or brand of broadhead.

ALIGN a broadhead with a precision arrow straightener. Place the nose cone of the head (just in front of the blades) on one set of rollers, the shaft a couple of inches behind the head on the other set of rollers, and press the bending lever just behind the broadhead.

How to Find the Balance Point of an Arrow

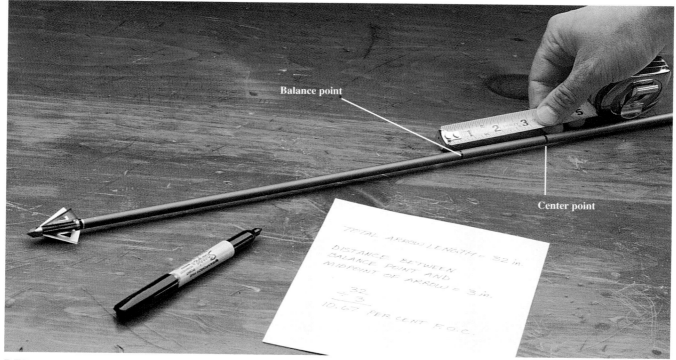

DETERMINE the balance point of an arrow by stabilizing in on the edge of a narrow object and measuring the distance between the center point and the balance point. Divide this number by the length of the arrow to arrive at the FOC (forward of center) balance percentage.

To figure balance point, first measure the arrow from nock to the tip of the broadhead, then mark the arrow shaft at the halfway point. Next, balance the arrow on a thin object, mark the point at which it balances and mark that point. Finally, measure the distance from the center mark and the balance point, and divide this distance by the total length of the arrow. For example, a 30-inch arrow that balances at the 12-inch point has a 10 percent FOC balance: [15 minus 12] divided by 30.

Balance point is governed primarily by head weight, though shaft weight and fletching also have an effect. If your arrows are significantly less than 10 percent FOC, then switch to heavier heads to move the FOC balance point forward. Or, if you like the lightweight heads you're shooting, you can switch to lighter shafts, or use smaller or lighter fletching to reduce the tail weight of the arrow.

Most traditional broadheads (opposite page) have a flat main blade, generally of welded steel. Flat blades like this are prone to bend, and they gain their strength primarily from the thickness of the blade. For adequate strength, most have a main blade of .040 inch or thicker, made of hardened steel. Many traditional heads have auxiliary, or "bleeder," blades, either pressed out of the main blade or inserted into a slot.

Modern, modular broadheads have a central column, or ferrule, and replaceable blades that lock into slots in the column. By their very structure, these blades resist bending better than do flat traditional heads, but their durability also depends on blade thickness. To reduce weight, some manufacturers reduce blade thickness, down to .015 inch in some cases, which makes the broadhead too fragile for practical big-game hunting. Generally, blades less than .020 inch thick will bend or break on impact with solid objects – like bone. For adequate durability, buy heads with blades between .020 and .030 inch thick. Most modern broadheads in this range have cutouts in the blades to reduce weight and surface area while maintaining strength.

Bowhunters often debate the penetrating qualities of chisel versus conical versus cut-to-tip broadheads. Conventional wisdom says cut-to-tip points penetrate better than other styles because they cut immediately on impact with an animal – a principle often demonstrated by slicing into a piece of leather using minimal force. In truth, however, conical or chisel points penetrate nearly as well as cut-to-tip broadheads when they strike an animal at full velocity. Conical heads, however, with their smooth, bullet shape, tend to deflect more easily than other styles of heads, especially on quartering shots. For this reason,

Broadhead Designs

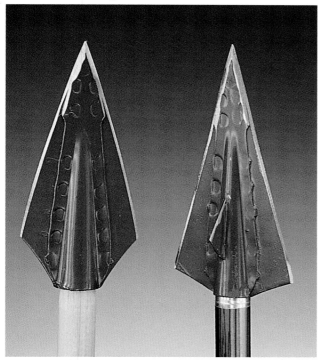

TRADITIONAL BROADHEADS usually have a main blade made of welded steel. Some traditional heads have smaller blades, called *bleeder blades* (right).

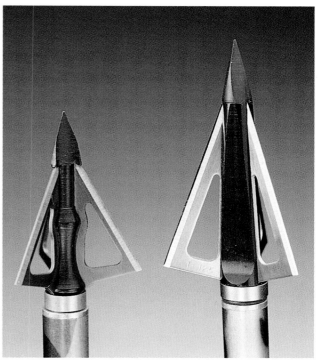

MODERN BROADHEADS are modular, consisting of a center column and replaceable blades.

Broadhead Tip Designs

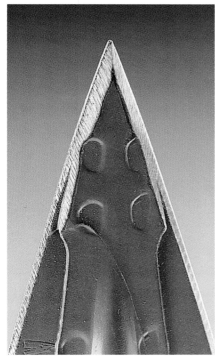

CUT-TO-TIP broadheads are sharpened right to the tip of the blade so they begin to cut the instant contact is made.

CHISEL-TIP broadheads have flattened surfaces on the tip of the head, which is usually attached to or is part of the ferrule.

CONICAL-TIP broadheads have a rounded tip that is part of the ferrule.

chisel tips have largely replaced conical tips on modular heads.

Penetration, of course, depends not only on tip shape but on blade sharpness. Blades can be dulled by dust and by pushing arrows into a quiver. To touch up slightly dulled blades, specialized sharpeners like Tru-Angle Hones®, which have the proper angle built into the hones, work very well. These are made for two, three and four-blade heads. The sharpeners with crossed steel or ceramic rods also can be used for touch-up work. For more severely dulled modular heads, replace all the blades with new, factory sharpened blades.

Traditional heads should first be filed to achieve the proper blade bevel, and they can then be sharpened on a stone by drawing the blade across the stone, much like sharpening a knife. Start with a coarse stone, and then finish up with a fine stone and a ceramic crock stick or leather strop. The important point in sharpening is to maintain a consistant angle along the length of the blade.

Some knife-sharpening systems, like the Lansky®, which employs a bracket to hold the blade at a fixed angle, prove ideal for sharpening fixed-blade broadheads.

Methods of Attaching Broadheads

ALUMINUM ARROWS use a threaded insert made of carbon or aluminum, into which the broadheads are screwed (left). To replace the head, use a broadhead wrench (right) to unscrew the old head and screw in the new broadhead.

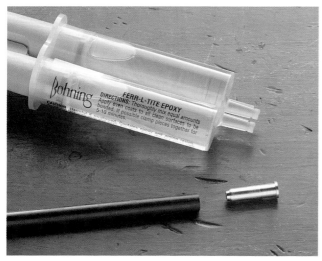

CARBON ARROWS use inserts which are glued into place with two-part epoxy for additional strength. This allows all standard broadhead designs to be used with carbon shafts. This was not the case when carbon arrows were first introduced. They originally required special outserts or broadheads that fit over the shaft.

SWAGING is an old concept gaining new popularity for weight reduction. Using a special swaging tool, pro shops can taper the end of an aluminum arrow (bottom), the same way as wood shafts are tapered. Swaged screw-in adapters (top) are also available. Traditional heads are then glued directly to this swage.

How to Sharpen Traditional Broadheads

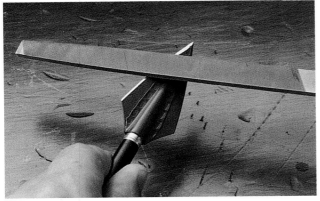

USE a broadhead file to flatten the bevel of the blade edges, using a series of forward strokes.

SPREAD a few drops of honing oil on a coarse sharpening stone. Place the edge of the blade near the front of the stone. Draw the blade back across the stone, as though trying to slice the oil off the stone.

WORK from the back end of the blade to the middle, and finally the tip, of the blade. Flip the blade over and hone the other side.

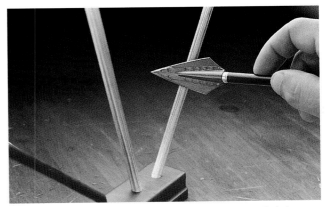

FINISH the blade edges by drawing them very lightly across a ceramic sharpening stick or leather strop.

How to Sharpen Modern Broadheads

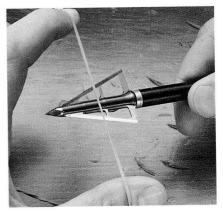

USE a hone to sharpen modern broadheads. Lay the head so two blades rest on the stone (left), with the ferrule in the groove. Stroke the blades across the stone, moving forward only. Rotate the arrow and make additional strokes to sharpen all blades. To finish-sharpen the blades, replace the stone block with a leather block (right), then draw the blades back across the leather. These hones are also available for traditional heads.

TEST for sharpness by drawing the cutting edge across a rubber band. The weight of the arrow alone will slice the rubber band if the broadhead is sufficiently sharp.

Bowsights

Bowhunters fall into two categories: instinctive or barebow shooters, and those who use mounted sights on their bows.

Good instinctive shooters aim using intuitive skills honed from hundreds of hours of practice. The eye and brain instinctively evaluate range and make automatic decisions on when to release. Instinctive shooters often compare their style to that used when hunting with a shotgun, a sport in which a hunter doesn't aim, but rather points and shoots. Instinctive bow shooting is similar. As you swing the bow into shooting position and concentrate on the target, you instinctively know when to release.

Some archers have great success with instinctive shooting, but for most hunters shooting a bow is more like shooting a rifle than a shotgun, since there is a single projectile that requires precise aiming. For the majority of bowhunters – especially compound bow shooters – a sighting system is considered essential equipment.

Sights are especially valuable for beginners, because they make it easier to analyze mistakes. When shooting instinctively, it's hard to know if a miss is caused by bad form or a faulty aim, but with a sighting system, you'll know your aim is on target and can concentrate on evaluating your form. Even Fred Bear, famous for his instinctive shooting, recommended sights to help beginners learn faster.

Sights can also help minimize target panic. Because the hunter must focus on the sight mechanism, he is distracted away from the animal – the cause of the psychological tension.

Bowsights come in a bewildering array of choices, as a glance at any archery supply catalog will demonstrate, and new variations and styles are offered every year. Whether you rely on simple pin sights or choose the latest in fiber-optic and laser-targeting technology, your selection is largely a matter of personal preference. No one style works best for everyone, so you'll need to try different sights until you find one that lets you shoot quickly and confidently. For most hunters, simple sights are the best choice; if you have to think too much when aiming, you'll lose many easy opportunities at game.

Bowsight technology changes too fast to catalog every style of bowsight a hunter is likely to encounter, but most will fall into one of the basic categories shown on these pages. In some states, electronic sighting systems are illegal, so always check hunting regulations in your area.

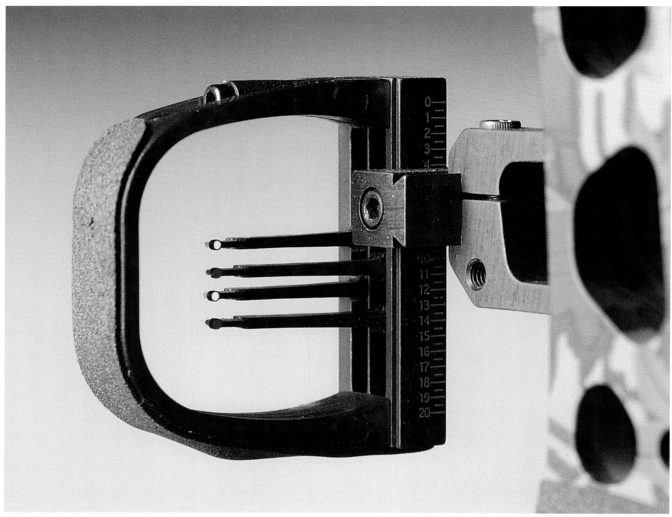

Double-channel fiber-optic sight

Fiber-Optic Sights

The most popular style bowsight is the fiber-optic sight. Fiber-optic sights gather existing light and channel it to the tip of the pin, where it transmits a small, brightly colored light. A number of different colored pins are available. Most hunters using fiber-optics use three to five sight pins. The pin guard helps protect the fibers which are somewhat more delicate than other types of sight pins. There are small lights available that help illuminate fiber-optic pins under low-light situations.

Pin Sights

MULTIPLE-PIN SIGHTS. Most pin sights have four or five pins that many hunters set in 10-yard increments for ranges between 10 and 50 yards. This configuration covers all situations and works especially well in still-hunting or stalking, where shooting distances can vary greatly.

If you choose a sight with multiple pins, make sure the sight offers adequate pin spacing. On slower bows, one pin channel will do. But if you're shooting at speeds faster than 230 feet per second, your sight must have two pin channels in order to position the pins close enough together. For better visibility, some hunters remove all but two pins – setting them at 20 and 40 yards, for example, then holding under or over for shots at intermediate ranges.

SINGLE-PIN SIGHTS. Sights that use a single pin can either be fixed or movable. Many hunters prefer the simplicity of a fixed single-pin sight for close-range shooting from a blind or stand when hunting deer or turkey. On a fast bow with a single pin set for 20 yards, you can aim almost dead on at any range out to 25 yards, which makes aiming simple, fast and efficient.

Pin sights can be either multiple-pin or single-pin (inset)

For shooting over longer, varied distances, a movable single-pin sight is a better choice. The biggest advantage of a movable pin is that you can always aim with your sight dead on the center of the target. Imagine you have a deer standing 35 yards away. With a multiple fixed-pin sight, you would have to frame the deer between your 30- and 40-yard pins; with a single fixed-pin sight, you'd have to place the pin over the deer or high on its back. But with a single, movable pin, you can adjust to the correct distance and center your pin on the deer's chest. Despite this advantage, however, the system has obvious drawbacks. In the excitement of hunting, you may forget to set the distance; and with game that is moving, you may not have time to adjust your sight.

One type of adjustable sight mounts to the bow with a mechanism that swivels smoothly up and down to adjust the sight to the proper setting. Most shooters tape yardage marks to the back of the sight for a quick reference point. The sight comes in sturdy plastic and machined aluminum models. You can lock the sight into any given yardage, say 20 yards for stand-hunting, or leave it free for quick changes at various distances.

Some of these sights have an optional mechanism that allows for quick adjustments with the index finger on your bow hand.

Another option is a single fixed-pin sight on a special mounting bracket that adjusts for different ranges. With adjustable scopes or rifle bars, you must raise your anchor point for close shooting and lower the anchor point for greater distances. Changing the anchor point may not be a problem if you use a release aid, but finger shooters who anchor in exactly the same spot each time may find these mounting brackets difficult to use.

Although modern bowsights are equipped with pin guards to protect the pins from damage, hunters should always take a practice shot before going into the woods to make sure that their sight or sight pins have not moved.

Cross-Hair Sights

The advantages of cross-hair style sights have made them almost as popular as pin sights. Rifle hunters in particular find it easier to aim with a cross hair because the sight picture resembles that of a rifle scope. Also, if you line up the vertical wire through the center of your target – e.g., the kill zone of a deer – you're virtually guaranteed correct windage, allowing you to focus strictly on elevation. Some archers shoot cross hairs without a peep, but if you get the string directly in front of your eye, it can obscure the vertical wire on the sight. For this reason, it's a good idea to add a peep sight, which allows you to look through the center of the string.

Like pin sights, cross-hair sights come in many varieties, including fixed single-point, adjustable single-point and multiple-point. Some variations combine a vertical wire with a standard pin or sliding beads. Adjustable cross-hair sights have a mechanism that adjusts the sight to the proper range; you can lock the sight into any given yardage or leave it free for quick changes at longer distances.

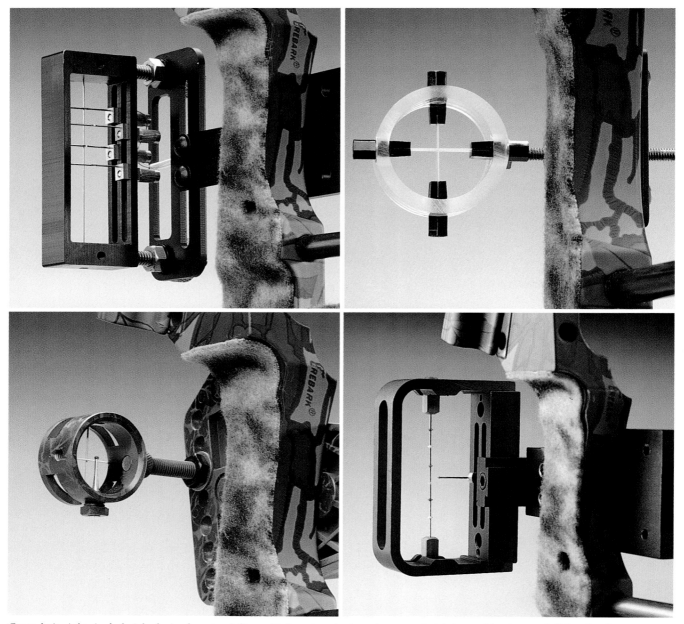

Cross-hair sights include (clockwise from top left): multiple-point, single-point, cross-hair/pin combination, and sliding bead

aim because the bright dot stands out vividly against virtually any target. They do, however, have drawbacks.

Most dot sights are electronic, which makes them illegal in some states, and as with any electronic device, the batteries can go dead. And the combined scope and mounting bracket can be fairly large and heavy. They're best suited for stand-hunting in low-light conditions and at known shooting distances.

Laser Sights

Laser sights could be considered a variation of the red-dot sight, although the dot is not seen inside a scope but is projected onto the target. Laser sights exploded onto the scene several years ago, creating a flurry of interest, but the device has several drawbacks that have caused enthusiasm to wane.

Like dot sights, laser sights are electronic and therefore illegal in some states. Because the beam pro-

Rifle-Bar Sights

Rifle-bar sights (above) have a rear V sight and a front bead sight mounted on a steel bar about a foot long. To aim, you center the front bead in the rear V, just as when aiming a rifle with open sights.

As proponents point out, the rifle-bar sight helps expose bad shooting habits, such as torquing of the bow, because the rear and front sights won't line up if your form is seriously out of whack. With a built-in rear sight, the rifle bar eliminates the need for a string peep. Like other single-point sights, rifle bars must be readjusted for different distances.

Dot Sights

Dot sights look like small rifle or pistol scopes. They have a bright ball, red in most cases, suspended in a blank background. Dot sights can ensure a quick

jects onto the target, intervening objects can "intercept" the beam. The strength of the beam depends on distance to the target, and because lasers are single-dot sights, you're limited in how far you can hold under or over a target; hold too far in either direction and the beam will not hit the target.

Visibility

A sight system that is hard to see in low-light situations – early morning hours or in the shadows of a dense forest – is of little use. For this reason, bowsight manufacturers are constantly developing and testing ways to improve the visibility on sights.

If you're buying a new sight, look for one with brightly painted heads or cross hairs that show up well in varied light conditions. If the heads of your sight pins are made of brass or another single-colored metal, consider painting them for greater visibility. Brass pins, in particular, tend to "flare" in bright sunlight, giving them a halo-like effect. To distinguish pins for various ranges, alternate colors, such as fluorescent orange and chartreuse. To paint your pins (below), first clean them thoroughly with

solvent, then apply white paint, either by dipping or spraying. When the white has dried, paint the pins various fluorescent colors, readily available at hobby stores.

Some excellent cross-hair sights have all-black wires, which can be painted the same way as described for pins. To highlight only the intersections of the wires – the aiming points – paint them with a fine brush. Or, if you're using spray paint, cut a small hole in a piece of paper and use the paper to mask off everything but the intersection of the wires.

Fluorescent plastic sight pins or cross hairs improve visibility in low light. Even brighter are fiber-optic sights. On these, long strands of brightly colored optical fibers gather external light and channel it to the tips of the fibers, which serve as the sight pins.

For all-around hunting, you can't beat fiber optics, although they do have a couple of limitations. Fiber-optic sights are not as durable as other styles. And in bright sunlight the glowing pins, cross hairs or dots may not show up well against the sunlit target. That's especially true when shooting from a dark area into bright light – from a dark antelope blind into open, sunlit sagebrush, for example. The shaded sight gathers very little light, and the pins are nearly invisible against a brightly lit target. Solid pins or black cross hairs work better under these conditions.

Electronically lighted sight pins are, of course, another option. Keep in mind that electronic devices can fail you and that they're illegal in some states. In addition, the Pope and Young Club will not record animals taken with any electronically equipped tackle. So, if you're interested in entering animals into the archery record book, stick with fiber optics.

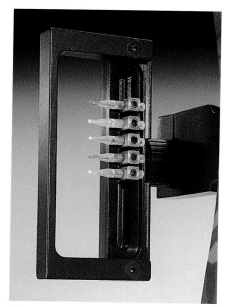

FIBER-OPTIC SIGHTS gather existing light and channel it to the end of the pin, where it glows brightly. Fiber optics are available on many types of pin and cross-hair sights.

ELECTRONIC SIGHTS include small battery-powered lights that shine onto standard pins or through fiber optics, and others with individually lighted pins. Others, like the dot and laser sights (p. 53), present a bright, electronic aiming dot.

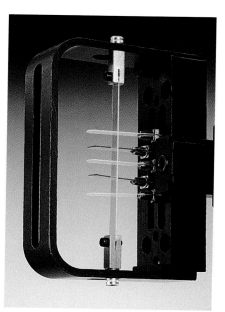

FLUORESCENT PLASTIC SIGHTS use cross hairs or sight pins made from brightly colored plastic to help improve visibility in low-light conditions.

Construction and Design

A broken sight can ruin a hunt, so put high priority on durability when selecting a bowsight. The simplest sights have a flat mounting bracket that screws onto the side of the bow. These sights are not very durable, because the bracket can be bent and the pins knocked out of line with a good blow from the side. If you opt for this inexpensive style, mount it on the inside of the handle – between the handle and the string, where it's well protected.

For a more reliable (and generally more expensive) alternative, look into a dovetail mount. Not only are machined dovetail mounts stronger by virtue of design and weight, but they're more versatile, too. You can quickly remove your sight for carrying in a bow case, and if you want to use different sights, say with pins for 3-D and cross hairs for hunting, you can easily alternate the two on one mounting bracket.

Also, insist on a good pin guard. On most cross-hair sights that's not a concern because the aiming wires are enclosed in a stout metal or tough plastic frame. But some pin sights have exposed pins, an invitation to disaster. Don't buy a sight without a rugged frame that fully protects the pins.

A sight must offer total vertical and horizontal adjustment. The higher your anchor point, the lower your sight must be set, and the lower your anchor point, the higher the sight. Some poorly designed sights simply won't adjust high or low enough to accommodate all shooting styles. Some also have inadequate lateral adjustment, so that when you screw the pins out to adjust for windage, they jam right up against the pin guard. These oversights are bad planning on the part of manufacturers. Make sure you buy a sight with adequate adjustment to accommodate your style.

Look also at the size and placement of screws. Sights with four or five sizes of allen screws, some microscopic in size and placed in unreachable positions, are tedious and frustrating to work on. For simplicity, buy a good sight with no more than two sizes of allen screws, all placed in easy-to-reach places. The best sights are easy to adjust, with independent mechanisms for windage and elevation so you can adjust one without altering the other.

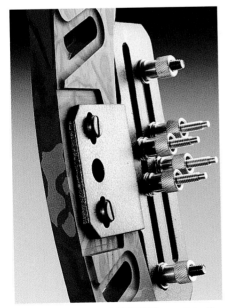

SCREW-ON BRACKETS consist of a flat piece of metal screwed to the bow. They are inexpensive, but not very durable.

DOVETAIL BRACKETS are solid and durable, and allow you to easily attach and remove the bowsight.

PIN GUARDS prevent the sight pins from being bent, broken or knocked out of alignment. Good pin guards are sturdy and enclose the pins without interfering with visibility.

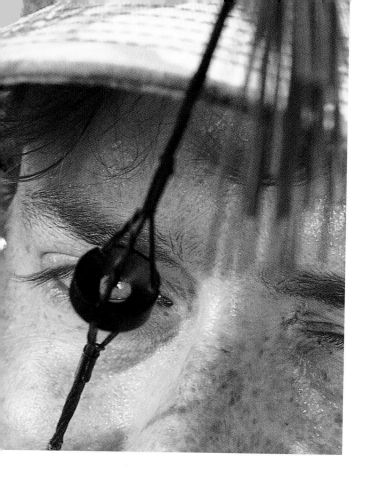

Peep Sights

A peep sight serves the same function as the rear sight on a rifle – to guarantee good alignment with the target. With a faulty rear sight, you can have the front sight precisely on the target and still miss badly.

Traditionally, the archer's "rear sight" has been his anchor point – the spot near his face where the string hand rests at full draw. If this anchor point is identical for each shot, the relationship between the shooter's eye and the front sight never varies, and aiming is no problem. But varying the anchor point by tiny fractions of an inch can cause your shot to be inches – or even feet – off the target.

The solution is the peep sight, a small ring with a viewing aperture, which is inserted between the strands of the bowstring. Inserting a peep sight ensures that you'll look through the string the same way every shot, which is especially important in awkward shooting positions, when you might anchor sloppily. If you use cross-hair sights, a peep is a useful tool, since without it the string can cover up the vertical wire in the sight. A peep won't guarantee you success, and it could even cost you an occasional shot. But bowhunting is a game of percentages,

and the odds favor the consistent accuracy produced by a peep sight.

To work properly, the peep sight must rotate so the hole faces your eye when you draw the bow. If not, you'll find your view blocked by a solid black mass – a disaster when you have a trophy animal standing within easy bow range. That's why some hunters refuse to use a peep. Certainly it's a legitimate concern, but it shouldn't deter you from trying a peep, because the problem can be solved in several ways.

FREE-FLOATING PEEP. With standard peeps, you have two ways to adjust peep rotation. One is to unstring your bow and turn the bowstring so the peep naturally lines up with your eye as you draw. To set a peep correctly, shoot a few times to see how the peep lines up. If it's turned to the side, unstring the bow and twist the string (p. 86) until the peep aligns correctly when you draw.

If you shoot with fingers, you may find it necessary to set the peep so it is turned a full 180 degrees away when the bow is relaxed. As you draw, the string will rotate far enough to align the peep hole with your eye. With a release aid, the string may rotate less, depending on how tightly your string is twisted. Twisting a string tightly, particularly with Fast Flight string material, tends to stabilize a peep sight well.

You also can adjust a free-floating peep by lifting strands of the string off one side of the peep and moving them to the other side. This eventually will change the torque on the peep and bring it into proper alignment. Splitting the string so half the strands are on each side of the peep does not ensure correct alignment; you may end up with as many as 12 strands on one side of the peep and as few as 6 on the other side. If your string is twisted tightly, using this adjustment method will be difficult.

SELF-ALIGNING PEEPS. On these peep sights, a rubber tube extends from the back of the peep to the face of the bow or to the cables. When you draw, the tube stretches tight, pulling the peep straight every time. In this sense, they're virtually foolproof. However, the tubing sometimes makes a slapping noise when you release, and it can break and slap you in the face or eye. Replace worn tubing occasionally to prevent breakage.

Other devices, such as string loops and metal loops, help align the peep sight the same way every time and ensure proper peep alignment (p. 70).

HORIZONTAL PEEP. Another peep style sits in the string horizontally, with the hole facing straight up and down. As you draw the bow, the changing angle of the string rotates the peep to a near-vertical position so you can see through the hole. With this system, it makes no difference how the string turns because you can always see through the hole. However, the peep doesn't come back in a completely vertical position, so you're always looking through the hole at a slant. In good light that doesn't matter, but in low light, it can hamper aiming.

HOLE SIZE. For hunting, the hole in a peep should be at least $1/8$ inch in diameter, preferably $3/16$ or $1/4$ inch to ensure that you can see through it even in low light and when it is not aligned perfectly. Free-floating peeps that sit vertically or horizontally in the string come back at a slant when you draw, which means you must look through the hole at an angle, and if the hole isn't large enough, you'll have trouble seeing through it. A large hole improves visibility, and it doesn't reduce accuracy, because your eye automatically centers the sight pin in the peep. If the hole in your peep is too small, drill it out

with a wood bit (above); most peeps are made of plastic or aluminum, which are easy to drill.

Some hunters prefer peeps that sit diagonally in the string, so that as the bow is drawn, the peep rotates to a perfectly vertical position and the shooter looks straight through the hole.

Types of Peep Sights

FREE-FLOATING PEEPS must be adjusted carefully so they align correctly with the eye when the bow is drawn.

SELF-ALIGNING PEEPS have a rubber tubing that attaches to the bow's cable or limb. When the bow is drawn, the tube pulls the peep into proper alignment.

HORIZONTAL PEEPS align correctly when the bow is drawn, but because they are positioned at an angle, the aperture appears smaller to the eye.

Accessories

B owhunters have a huge assortment of accessories from which to choose. Some are essential, others are helpful and some you may find unnecessary. No two people will agree completely on which accessories are necessary or which equipment works best. One person's help is another's hindrance, which is why no one can prescribe an exact recipe for the perfect hunting setup. The following pages present the pros and cons of common accessories, but leave the ultimate decision up to you.

Some criteria apply universally when choosing accessories. First and foremost is durability, because nothing can ruin a hunt faster than broken tackle. Your equipment also must be silent; a noisy, rattling bow is an obvious liability. Finally, your accessories must be easy to use – fighting with complicated adjustments and instructions can turn anyone off of archery.

Mechanical Release Aids

Only a few years ago, virtually all hunters held and released their bowstrings using fingers, but today it is estimated that at least 75 percent of all bowhunters use mechanical release aids. Release aids are no passing fad; in target archery, finger-release shooters find it impossible to compete with release-

aid shooters, and the two groups are placed in separate classes.

Why are release aids so effective? First, a finger-release archer grips the string across a broad area with two or three fingers. This broad connection with multiple points of contact makes it difficult to maintain the identical form for each shot. A release aid, by contrast, grips the string at one tiny point, so the string slips away smoothly, shot after shot, with little variation.

Second, a mechanical aid introduces the element of surprise to your release. For best accuracy, you should be totally surprised when the bow releases. When shooting with fingers, it's hard to achieve total surprise because the decision to open your fingers is a conscious choice. The result can be erratic accuracy. By contrast, when you slowly squeeze the trigger on a release aid, you'll truly be surprised when the bow goes off. This is especially helpful for preventing or curing target panic and other shooting problems.

Under ideal conditions – at the target range on a calm day – the difference in accuracy and consistency may seem insignificant, but it becomes a major factor when you're brittle with cold or numbed with fatigue. At these moments, your fingers may let you down, but a mechanical release won't. The outcome of many hunts often comes down to one shot, and a release aid can help make that shot count.

That's not to say release aids are perfect. As with any other method, learning to shoot well with a release aid takes practice. Punching the trigger or

Release Methods

FINGER-RELEASE SHOOTERS have the meaty portion of two or three fingers on the bowstring, making it difficult to achieve an identical smooth release for each shot.

RELEASE AIDS grip the string at one tiny point, making it much easier to duplicate the same style, shot after shot.

MECHANICAL RELEASE STYLES include the wrist-strap (left), concho (center) and finger-held (right).

flinching with a release aid can lead to worse shooting than a bad finger release. You must learn to squeeze much like a hunter squeezes the trigger on a bench-rest rifle. Like any mechanical device, a release aid can fail. In extreme cold, moisture can freeze and lock up the release mechanism, and dirt or rust can jam a release aid, making it useless. Good maintenance can help prevent these problems (opposite page).

STYLE VARIATIONS. Mechanical release aids come in three basic styles: wrist-strap, concho and finger-held.

A wrist-strap release attaches directly to the wrist, leaving your fingers loose and relaxed. Because it buckles to your lower arm, there is little chance of losing a wrist-strap release. Most models have either caliper jaws or opposing ball bearings that lock in front of the string, and most are triggered with an index-finger trigger. Because you must attach the release to the string just before you shoot, wrist models can cause an excited hunter to fumble when hurrying for a shot.

A concho release aid has a head similar to that on wrist-strap models, but instead of a strap, it features a tube or grip that is held in the palm of your hand. Some models have a flat plate at the back to prevent your hand from slipping off the grip.

A hand-held release is T-shaped, with a rotating head attached at 90 degrees to a finger bar. Most shooters hold the release with the index finger on one side of the head, and the third and fourth fingers on the other side. Many finger-held models can be clipped

onto the string well before the shot; to keep the release aid from sliding down the string, either clamp a nock set or eliminator button just below it, or attach the release aid to a string loop (p. 70). Unless you tie it to your wrist, a finger-held release can be easy to misplace.

BOWSTRING ATTACHMENT. Most wrist-strap and concho releases, and some finger-held releases, grip the bowstring with either caliper jaws or opposing ball bearings that lock in front of the string. These types are popular with hunters because they're easy to operate. Pushing the trigger forward locks the jaws around the string and pulling the trigger back releases it – welcome simplicity in the excitement of hunting. In essence, this style provides a built-in safety – while drawing the bow, you simply hold your finger behind the trigger to keep it locked, and then slip your finger in front of the trigger to shoot.

Other attachment methods also are used, especially on finger-held release aids. Some models have a swiveling pin that locks in front of the string, others have a rotating sear. Probably the most popular among target archers is the rope release, which attaches to the string with a short rope loop. All of these styles can be used for hunting, though they are not as quick or simple to use as the caliper-style head.

TRIGGERING. Most hunters use release aids triggered with the index finger, probably because it resembles the familiar sensation of shooting a rifle. Index-finger triggers can, however, aggravate some

Release Attachment Variations

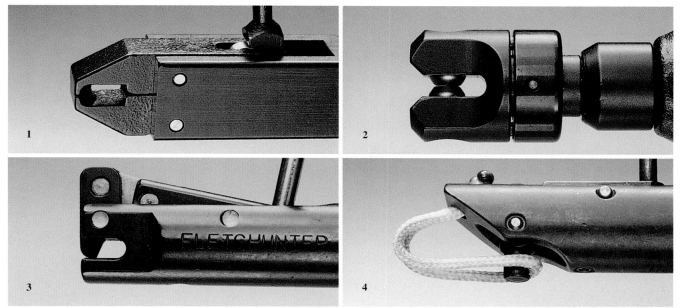

STRING-ATTACHMENT VARIATIONS include: (1) caliper, (2) ball-bearing, (3) rotating sear and (4) rope loop.

shooting problems. Because the index finger is sensitive, an archer may begin to anticipate when the release aid will go off, and this anticipation can lead to flinching or trigger punching, serious threats to accuracy. In many cases, the solution is simply

Thumb-trigger release

to switch to a release aid triggered with the less-sensitive thumb or little finger, reintroducing the element of surprise to the release.

Because accurate shooting is a product of relaxation, some archers find they can shoot better with a release that fires when the hand is relaxed rather than tightened. With this style, you squeeze the trigger while drawing the bow, and shoot by relaxing the trigger.

Another style releases only when the trigger is squeezed slowly and smoothly. If you punch the

Slow-squeeze trigger

trigger on this device, the release simply locks up, forcing you to let down and reset the trigger.

Some specialized release aids have no trigger at all, but are fired by increasing pressure on the string. After clipping the release to the string, you draw and aim. As you continue to pull with your back, the increasing pressure triggers the release. This device teaches you to pull with your back and to accept the element of surprise.

USE AND MAINTENANCE. Using a release must be automatic and second nature. Practice nocking an arrow and locking the release on the string with your eyes closed to learn to do it by feel. And shoot a lot. Regular practice builds proficiency.

In dry weather, where dust and dirt are the enemies, wash the release thoroughly with solvent to eliminate all oil. In wet weather, oil your release regularly to keep it from rusting. In the field, carry a small brush (an old toothbrush) to scrub dirt or debris out of the release aid. Most important, always carry a spare. That's the only absolute guarantee against loss and malfunction.

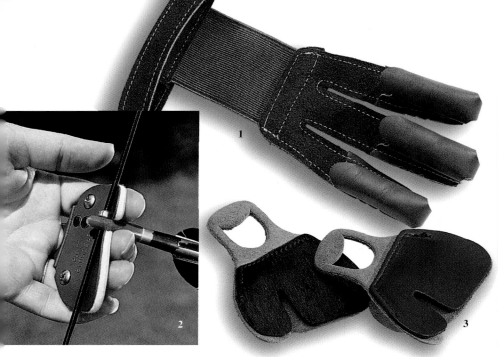

FINGER-RELEASE ACCESSORIES include: (1) shooting glove, (2) plastic tab, (3) hair-off and hair-on tabs and (4) finger spacer used to prevent pinching of the arrow when at full draw.

Finger-Release Accessories

Archers who release with their fingers can improve their performance with shooting gloves and other accessories.

SHOOTING GLOVES. At one time the shooting glove was the accepted method for protecting fingers during a shot, and it's still used by many traditional archers. Most shooting gloves are made of leather, with three finger stalls and a leather strap to hold the stalls in place. It's probably the fastest shooting method, because you grip the string directly with your fingers and can feel your way through the entire shot process.

However, shooting gloves do have drawbacks. Over time, the finger stalls develop grooves that inhibit a smooth release (right). With too much shooting, your fingers can develop grooves, too, a painful problem until you build up some major calluses. During wet weather, or when you're sweating hard, the leather stalls get soggy and can slip off your fingers during a shot. Finally, because your fingers are all working independently, you have to develop a flawlessly relaxed string release for consistent accuracy.

FINGER TABS. A finger tab is a simple leather or plastic pad held in place with a leather, plastic or rubber ring around the middle finger. Among finger-release shooters, tabs have all but replaced shooting

gloves because they offer a higher degree of shooting consistency. In effect, the tab molds your fingers into a single unit, ensuring a more consistent release, and because many tabs are padded, they reduce the finger pain sometimes caused by prolonged shooting. Because a tab hangs loose, your skin can breathe, eliminating the problem of sweaty, slippery fingers. Plastic tabs are affected much less by wet weather and sweat than are leather shooting gloves. During cold weather, a tab can be worn over a wool glove with little effect on accuracy.

Leather tabs are available in two styles: one with hair on the outside surface; the other, with no hair. When new, a hair-on tab allows the bowstring to slide smoothly across the surface during release, but as the hair wears off, the tab loses its efficiency. For this reason, many archers prefer a hairless leather tab that stays consistent over time.

Plastic tabs have a slick surface that ensures a consistent, smooth release. And although they don't have the natural feel of a leather tab, plastic tabs are unaffected by wet weather.

FINGER SPACERS. Commonly called a "can't pinch," a finger spacer enhances the effectiveness of a finger tab by preventing the shooter from pinching the arrow nock, which can cause painful blisters as well as affect your accuracy. Some archers pinch the nock so badly at full draw that they severely bend the arrow by pressing it down against the arrow rest. At release, the arrow recoils as it straightens out, beginning an unnatural oscillation that can spoil your accuracy. A finger spacer helps eliminate this problem.

Arm Guards and Chest Protectors

ARM GUARDS. Nothing can spoil a beginning archer's enthusiasm quicker than painful string burns on the arm. An arm guard protects the forearm and wrist from string slap and is essential gear, especially for novices. Arm guards generally are made of leather or plastic. Leather models conform to the arm better and last forever, but ventilated plastic models reduce sweating under the arm guard by allowing the skin to breathe.

With practice, an archer can learn to hold the bow arm to prevent string slap on bare skin. But arm guards are still valuable as a means of holding clothing out of the way of the string. Even experienced archers should wear an arm guard, because if the string hits a loose shirt cuff or bulky coat sleeve, the arrow won't hit the mark.

CHEST PROTECTORS. Like an arm guard, a chest protector can help hold loose or bulky shirts or coats out of the way of the bowstring. Especially popular with female archers, the protector consists of a ventilated plastic shield with shoulder and back straps that hold it in place over the chest.

Arrow Rests

As the last major contact point before an arrow leaves the bow, the arrow rest affects arrow spine value and controls clearance – two crucial variables governing good arrow flight. That's why arrow rest selection is so critical, and why you should never skimp on an arrow rest to save a few dollars.

A good arrow rest must hold a nocked arrow securely in place and also allow for good clearance as the arrow leaves the bow. It must be dependable, durable, accurate, quiet, reasonably easy to adjust and easy to use under hunting conditions.

Arrows shot with fingers behave differently from arrows shot with a release aid, and the two shooting styles require different types of arrow rests.

When an arrow is released with fingers, the string is thrust drastically to the side, which bends the arrow and starts a pattern of oscillation, similar to the motion of a salmon swimming upstream. With a right-handed shooter, for example, the fingers push the string and the nock of the arrow to the left at the moment of release, and the middle of the arrow bellies

Arm guard and chest protector

to the right. About halfway through the power stroke of the string, the arrow nock swings right and the arrow bellies to the left. And just before it leaves the string, the arrow bellies right again, and the nock swings to the left, out around the bow handle and arrow rest. If the arrow is properly spined and the rest is set correctly, the arrow remains in contact with the rest for only 6 to 8 inches before reaching free flight, with little or no fletching contact.

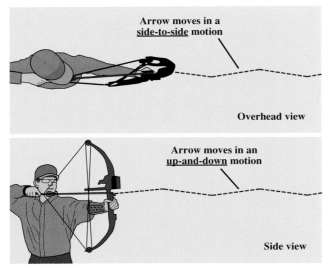

Arrow moves in a side-to-side motion

Overhead view

Arrow moves in an up-and-down motion

Side view

Overhead view of finger-release arrow (top), and side view of mechanical-release arrow

By contrast, a release aid lets the string go straight forward rather than pushing it to the side, and as a result the arrow bends much less on the power stroke. The arrow still oscillates, but generally in a vertical plane, with a motion more like that of a porpoise than a salmon. Most important, the arrow remains in contact with the rest for its full length. This is why release-aid shooters need different rest styles than do finger-release shooters.

FINGER-RELEASE ARROW RESTS. When shot with fingers, arrows tend to leap out around the bow. For this reason, the best choice is a "shoot-around" rest, which is open on one side and won't obstruct the sideways oscillation of the arrow.

The bow shelf is the most rudimentary shoot-around rest. It's obviously durable, and when covered with leather, moleskin or other soft material, it's also quiet. But you must use arrows with feather fletchings when shooting off the shelf – plastic vanes bounce off, giving you terrible arrow flight. And shooting off the shelf offers little flexibility for tuning your bow. You can change nocking point height, vary spine value of your arrows, and alter brace height of your bow, but that's about it. Many recurve and longbow archers shoot off the shelf, but virtually all compound shooters use a raised rest.

At one time, most compound bows came factory-equipped with solid plastic rests, which are simple, durable and cheap. *Solid rests* have some of the same drawbacks as shooting off the shelf. Contact between the arrow fletching and rest will throw an arrow off. By causing drag on the arrow, a solid rest can even reduce arrow speed. With many solid plastic rests, contact is so severe you'll see black streaks of plastic on the vanes of the arrows. Using feathers can minimize this effect, but it is impossible to avoid with plastic vanes. For best accuracy, a solid rest must be mounted on a plate that can be adjusted laterally for proper alignment.

The spring rest, often called a *springy*, is reasonably adjustable. You can move it in and out for center-shot adjustment, and you can use different weight springs – 15-, 20-, 25-ounce – to alter spine value of your arrow. To get the best arrow clearance, you can clip back the spring end so it is just long enough to hold an arrow; many archers bend the tip up to hold the arrow in place. To silence the rest, you can slip Teflon tubing over the end of the spring. Springy rests are popular among hunters for their durability, although it is possible to snag the spring and bend it.

The *flipper/plunger,* which consists of a movable arrow-support arm and a spring-loaded plunger or pressure button at the side, has become the most popular rest among finger-release shooters. Because the arm moves easily out of the way, the flipper/plunger gives good arrow flight with both feathers and vanes. Even though vanes may brush the support arm, there is rarely any problem with severe wobbling.

Both lateral position (center shot) and spring tension of the side plate or cushion plunger are adjustable; so, in essence, they change the spine value of the arrow. This allows you to fine-tune your bow to accommodate many combinations of shaft, fletching and broadhead.

Flipper/plunger rests are fairly dependable, although the arm can be snagged and bent, and the plunger can freeze in winter. The flipper/plunger offers the best all-around tuning potential and arrow flight for finger-release shooters. To improve quietness, cover the arm with a Teflon sleeve.

RELEASE-AID RESTS. Some hunters shoot the flipper/plunger with a release aid, but this practice is not advised. Because the arrow doesn't flex out around the rest, as it does when shooting with fingers, there is usually significant contact between the fletching and the arrow rest. In addition, the support arm on a flipper/plunger doesn't offer the vertical flex necessary when shooting with a release aid. For

Arrow Rests for Use by Finger Shooters

BOW SHELF RESTS are used primarily on traditional bows. The arrow lies directly on the shelf, which is often covered with fleece or another material to protect the arrow and dampen sound.

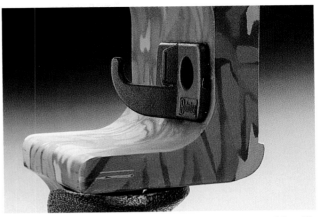

SOLID PLASTIC RESTS are attached to the bow with self-adhesive backing. They are inexpensive, but because they are not adjustable, erratic arrow flight can be a problem.

"SPRINGY" RESTS feature a coiled spring that supports the arrow. They can be easily adjusted for center shot.

FLIPPER-PLUNGER RESTS have an adjustable spring-loaded plunger attached to an arm, or "flipper," that supports the arrow. This style is very popular because of its adjustablility.

Arrow Rests for Use with Release Aids

LAUNCHER RESTS can be precisely adjusted. Launcher rests offer great fletch clearance, making them popular with archers using carbon arrows.

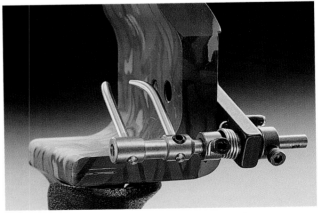

PASS-THROUGH RESTS are designed so the arrow fletching passes through the arms of the rest, allowing for truer arrow flight.

Arrow Rest Tips

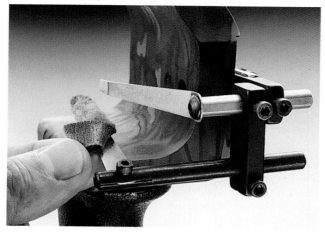

ADDING moleskin, Teflon, or heat-shrink to a rest makes it much quieter, so game animals will not hear the arrow being drawn and released.

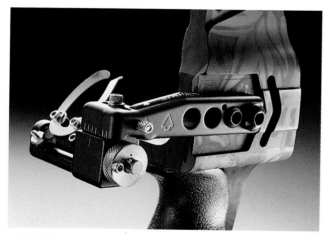

ADJUST center shot and arm height in small increments – a task made easier if you use a rest equipped with micro-adjustability and indexing.

TURN arrow nocks so the fletching clears the arms of a pass-through rest. If the fletching hits the rest as the arrow is released, the arrow will fly erratically.

these reasons, most release-aid shooters prefer two other styles – *launchers* and *pass-through* rests.

Most launchers consist of a single arm with a V-shaped end that cradles the arrow. When shot, the arrow shaft slides along this V, and the fletching passes to the sides of the launcher arm. Although many target archers use launchers because they are easy to tune and give good fletching clearance, launchers have drawbacks for hunting. Because the arrow is simply balanced on top of the rest, it can easily fall off in hunting situations. And with many styles, it is difficult to achieve the necessary silence for hunting.

Among hunters who use release aids, pass-through rests are preferred. With this style, the arrow is cradled between two arms, or between an arm and a plunger button, and the fletching passes through the rest rather than around it, as it does on other types of rests. Most pass-through rests cradle the arrow securely to keep it from falling off in hunting situations.

Pass-through rests can be moved in and out for center-shot adjustment, and arm spacing can be varied to accommodate different shaft diameters. Some pass-through rests have independent vertical and horizontal settings, which makes for tedious adjustment. Rests with micro-tuning features are easiest to adjust, although they have more moving parts that could rattle loose. With a pass-through rest, you may need to turn the nocks on your arrows to ensure that the fletching will clear the rest cleanly.

High-quality models are durable and easy to silence for hunting. Prong styles can be silenced with shrink tubing or by wrapping moleskin around the prongs. Styles with wider, flat arms can be silenced by applying moleskin or stick-on carpeting to the arms. Without some material to cushion the arrow shaft, even the faint noise of the arrow shaft sliding across the rest can spook your quarry.

Overdraws

An overdraw has one simple function – to extend the rest behind the handle of the bow – and it has one purpose – to allow you to shoot arrows shorter than your actual draw length. For example, if your actual draw length measures 32 inches, you can, with an overdraw, shoot 27- or 28-inch arrows while still drawing the string 32 inches.

Archers with naturally short draw length – 28 inches or less – rarely need an overdraw, because these hunters can choose from a wide selection of suitable arrow shafts. But for archers with long draw lengths,

OVERDRAWS allow an archer to shoot arrows shorter than his draw length. Shooting shorter, lighter arrows increases arrow speed.

an overdraw does offer benefits. A hunter with a draw length over 30 inches shooting a heavy bow has few shaft options, other than to use stiff, relatively heavy shafts. By adding an overdraw, however, this hunter can shoot shorter, lighter arrows, which is the easiest way to increase arrow speed by as much as 20 feet per second.

If you decide to try an overdraw, remember two things. First, an overdraw is not well suited to shooting with fingers. With an overdraw extending the arrow rest to the back, the distance between the

string and the arrow rest is reduced. During release, the nock is still on the string as the fletching passes the rest (left). With a release aid, this causes no problem, because the arrow is moving straight forward. But with a finger release, which causes side-to-side oscillation, the string can drive the shaft

of the arrow sideways into the rest. Without adequate space between the string and rest, the arrow doesn't have adequate time to straighten out before the fletching passes the arrow rest.

Second, on bows with a low brace height, the cables may hit the back of a long overdraw. If the brace height of the bow is less than 6 inches, you may need to stick with a short overdraw, or use no overdraw at all. A bow should have at least 2 inches between the cables and overdraw shelf (or arrow rest) to ensure adequate clearance when shooting.

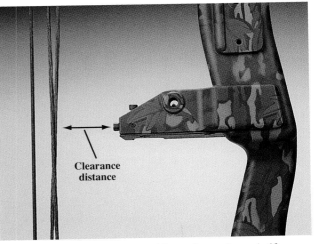

CLEARANCE between the cables and overdraw shelf or arrow rest should be at least 2 in. Make sure to measure this distance if you are shooting a bow with a short brace height.

Quivers

When selecting a quiver to carry your arrows and broadheads, you have three basic styles from which to choose: bow quivers, hip quivers and back quivers. Regardless of the style, a quiver must hold the arrows in a ready-to-use position; it must hold them securely to prevent damage to the arrows; it must be quiet; and, for safety, it must cover the broadheads completely and hold the shafts securely.

BOW QUIVERS. Due to its convenience, the bow quiver has been by far the most popular style since the 1950s. With a bow quiver, the arrows and bow become one convenient unit.

In picking a bow quiver, durability and solidity must come first, because a poorly made quiver will rattle and vibrate with every shot, spooking game and causing you endless irritation. The broadhead hood must be riveted or screwed solidly to the mounting bracket so it doesn't rattle, and must encase the broadheads completely in foam, both to prevent rattling and to ensure that you won't cut your fingers on partially exposed broadheads.

The shaft gripper bar also must be solidly attached to the mounting bracket, and the gripper slots must hold the arrows securely to prevent them from rattling or falling out. The broadhead hood and shaft grippers should be far enough apart to prevent the fletchings from rattling together with each shot; ideally, the grippers should hold the arrows just above the fletching. Small-diameter carbon arrows require special narrow grippers.

Two-piece models have separate hoods and shaft grippers. Some models are secured to the bow using the limb bolts, while others bolt onto the outside of the limb pockets. If you pick a one-piece quiver, make sure it's compatible with the components of your bow, such as the sight and cable guard. If you'll be shooting with the bow quiver attached, buy a model that screws solidly to the bow.

Quick-detach models are often used by stand-hunters, who carry their arrows in the quiver while walking, but remove the quiver once they arrive on stand. Shooting with a quick-detach quiver still attached to the bow is not advised, since they almost always make noise.

Eight-arrow quivers have become almost standard, especially in backcountry hunting, because a hunter can fill the quiver with enough arrows for several days of hunting. However, given the heavy weight of most compound bows, some hunters prefer a lighter, four-arrow quiver. In most situations, four arrows are more than enough for a day's hunting.

Does a bow quiver hurt accuracy? Although it does place more weight on one side of the bow, skewing the balance slightly, most archers find that a bow quiver does not hinder accuracy. Theoretically, the balance of the bow should change as arrows are removed from the quiver, but again, few hunters find this to be a significant problem.

HIP QUIVERS. Among target archers, belt quivers have always been the favorite style, perhaps because they can hold a notebook, binoculars and other items, in addition to arrows. But for hunters, the hip quiver nearly died with the advent of the bow quiver in the 1950s. Then, in the 1980s, hip quivers began to make a strong return to bowhunting. This new-found popularity was fueled largely by growing interest in bow tuning and pinpoint accuracy; some archers believed they could achieve finer accuracy shooting without a bow quiver to disrupt balance.

Good hip quivers have a broadhead hood and rubber shaft grippers much like those on good bow quivers. Some can be tied against your leg at the bottom to prevent flopping. Make sure the arrows are easy to retrieve, and that the fletching ends of the arrows don't get in the way when you walk or draw your bow. Many hip quivers are covered with fleece or other soft material for added quietness.

BACK QUIVERS. The same qualities required of bow and hip quivers – reliable broadhead protection, secure shaft grippers, solid construction and, quietness – also apply to back quivers. The original back quiver was little more than an open leather tube slung across the back with a shoulder strap. It held lots of arrows and allowed a longbow shooter to grab and fire arrows in a hurry, but had few other virtues. Tube-style back quivers allow arrows to rattle around and fall out – a serious safety hazard. Tube quivers are still seen around the target range, but rarely are used by hunters.

By contrast, modern back quivers are adjustable, with foam pads at each end that sandwich arrows lengthwise. Fletchings as well as broadheads are protected, and the shafts are held tightly to prevent any movement and noise. Most of these quivers have two padded shoulder straps and are worn like backpacks. Several versions have small packs built directly onto the quiver, and are ideal for short overnight trips in the field.

Types of Quivers

Shaft grippers

Quick-detach bow quiver

Arrow hood

Fixed bow quiver

Hip quiver

Back quiver

3-D target quiver

String Accessories

STRING LOOP. Hunters using release aids often find it helpful to tie a short piece of rope around the bowstring to form a loop ½ to ¾ inch long (below). The release aid is then attached to this loop rather than directly to the bow-string. The string loop has become increasingly popular with both hunters and tourna-ment archers for several rea-sons. It eliminates the string wear often caused by metal-jaw release aids, and by centering the release aid directly behind the arrow nock, it ensures that the force on the arrow is straight forward. In the opin-ion of many hunters, a string loop gives better broadhead flight. A finger-held release aid can be attached to the string loop ahead of time, which can save valuable seconds when you need to shoot quickly.

Metal loops offer an alternative to the rope loop. They're easier to use, because you simply sand-

String silencer

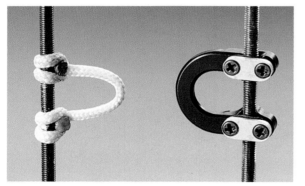

Rope string loop (left) and metal string loop (right)

wich the string between the two halves and screw them together. Unlike rope loops, however, a metal loop can be be torqued to twist the string, and it may cause noise if it clicks against the release aid.

NOCK SETS. Some hunters wrap extra serving thread around the string to form the nocking point, but most archers now use commercial nock sets. The simplest nock sets are a clamp-on metal version. Some styles have a little wing to keep the string from rotating, which assures that the peep sight will come back straight.

Nock set

When you use a release aid, upward pressure is exerted on the nocked arrow (unless a string loop is used). For this reason, archers using release aids

without a string loop find it necessary to reinforce the nocking point to keep it from sliding up on the string. Some archers wrap dental floss or serving string above the nocking point, or you can simply clamp two nock sets together, one above the other, to pre-vent slippage.

Because a release aid pushes hard against the nock of an arrow, some archers put a rubber O-ring, or *eliminator button*, on the string below the arrow nock as a cushion between the release aid and the arrow. And archers who use a finger-held release aid clipped to the string sometimes place a second nock set below the release aid to keep it from sliding down the string.

KISSER BUTTONS. The kisser button, a small plastic disk served into the bowstring, serves the same purpose as a peep sight – to guarantee a consis-tent anchor point and sight picture. At full draw, the disc is set to touch the archer's lip (thus the name *kisser*) in exactly the same place every time. Many target archers use kissers, and some hunters use them too, either in place of, or in addition to, a peep sight.

Kisser button

Using a kisser button

STRING SILENCERS. String vibration can cause excessive noise with each shot, but it's easily dampened with string silencers. The most common are *spider legs*, thin strips of rubber resembling the rubber skirt on a fishing lure. One small silencer, about 6 inches from each end of the string, should be adequate.

Silencers made of yarn or fleece also work well, although they absorb moisture and can actually mold if not dried periodically.

Types of Nock Sets

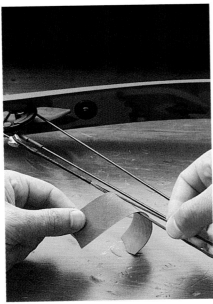

STRING ACCESSORIES include: (1) single nock set for finger shooters, (2) double nock set for release shooters, (3) extra serving thread to secure nock point, (4) additional nock set below nocking point and (5) O-ring below nock set to provide a cushion between the release aid and the arrow nock.

How to Attach a String Silencer

DIVIDE the string about 6 inches from the end, using your fingers, then insert a piece of silencer ¹/₂- to ³/₄-inch-wide through the string. Use a bow press to relax tension on the string, if necessary.

TIE a granny knot in the silencer around the string to keep it from slipping.

PULL the silencing material tight and cut it off near the ends, using a sharp knife or scissors to separate the individual strands.

Hunting stabilizer

Rubber damper

Stabilizers

Stabilizers can be divided into two categories – target and hunting. Target stabilizers, which consist of a bar up to 3 feet long and V bars to the side for balance, are not practical for hunting. But short, compact hunting stabilizers have become very popular. Many of these are segmented for easy length and weight adjustment.

A stabilizer attached to a bow does three things – adds weight, helps balance a bow and absorbs vibration.

In theory, the increased weight of a stabilizer can improve accuracy simply by increasing the inertia of the bow. When shot, a bow naturally reacts by moving one way or another. Adding weight reduces this movement and improves the potential accuracy of the bow. In practice, however, most compound bows equipped with a quiver and full accessories already weigh 6 pounds or more, which is heavy enough to ensure good accuracy. Adding additional weight may slightly improve your accuracy, but for most hunters the benefit is canceled by the added fatigue of carrying around extra weight.

A stabilizer also helps balance a bow. Ideally, a bow should stand straight up in your hand or tip forward after the shot. Many bows with straight or reflexed handles do just that, and a stabilizer is not needed. Bows with deflexed risers, on the other hand, often tip backward so sharply that the top limb will almost hit you in the head – adding a long overdraw aggravates the problem. A forward-extending sight can help counter this weight, but it's often not enough. By experimenting with stabilizers of various lengths and weights, you can balance any bow to stand upright after every shot.

Finally, a stabilizer can absorb excessive vibration. On bows with soft cams, this isn't necessarily a problem, and a stabilizer may not be needed. But many hard cams send virtual shock waves of vibration through the limbs and handle of a bow with every shot. To help with this problem, hunters can add a small rubber damper (left) to each bow limb to help absorb vibration. A stabilizer also absorbs some of this vibration, making the bow quieter and potentially extending its life. Some stabilizers have an internal hydraulic piston or rubber bushings specifically designed to absorb vibration and to reduce hand shock.

Cable Guard and Slides

The cable guard, which holds the cables to the side to prevent arrow fletching from touching the cables (right), comes standard on all compound bows. However, the friction of the cables against the rod of the cable guard can cause noise and can create wear on the cables. For this reason, most hunters attach a cable slide to the rod of the cable guard.

Cable slides (right) come in several styles. Simple plastic slides work well enough and weigh only 30 to 40 grains, but they sometimes squeak on a metal rod, especially if the rod gets wet. Teflon cable slides are silent, although they'll eventually wear out. Roller cable slides roll smoothly up and down the cable guard without noise. Some, however, are rather heavy – 200 grains or more. And roller slides may slam into the back of an overdraw if there is inadequate clearance between the cables and the overdraw.

Wrist Slings

Shooting correctly, with a relaxed bow hand and total surprise when the bow goes off, you're bound to drop the bow occasionally. Enter the wrist sling (right). This sling, made of a rope loop or leather strap, attaches below the grip and loops over the wrist. It allows you to keep your hand loose throughout the shot without worrying about dropping the bow. The purpose of the sling is to catch the bow; the sling should not be tight enough to affect your shot.

Moleskin

To prevent an arrow from clicking on the bow, cover the entire bow shelf, overdraw bracket and sight window with moleskin (below) or a similar adhesive-backed product.

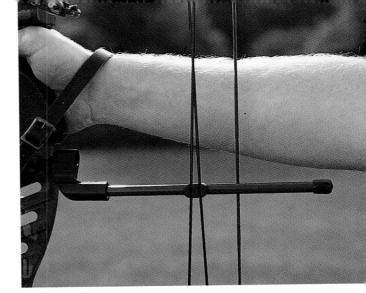

Cable guard

Cable slides include: (1) plastic, (2) Teflon and (3) roller

Wrist sling

Hard bow case and soft bow case (inset)

Bow Cases

A good compound bow is a finely crafted precision hunting tool, yet many archers think nothing of hanging it in a vehicle gun rack exposed to direct sun or tossing it in the bed of a pickup. After spending hundreds of dollars and many hours tuning and sighting in a bow, why ruin it by storing it so carelessly? A bow sitting exposed in a car parked in the sun can be ruined in just a few hours by heat causing its laminations to separate.

Protect your investment by storing your bow in a good bow case. For general hunting, a soft case padded with foam offers good protection and convenience. You can slip a bow in and out easily and it provides adequate protection, so long as you don't throw heavy objects like a spare tire or deer carcass onto it.

A soft case can even be used as airline luggage. Spread the case out flat and lay a thick layer of clothing on one side. Place your bow on the clothing, then cover the bow with another layer of clothes and zip up the case. Pad the bow as thickly as possible for maximum protection, but not so thickly as to stress the zipper. If you plan to use a soft case as luggage, buy one with a heavy metal zipper; weak nylon zippers can come apart. Most soft cases have exterior pockets to store additional items.

If you travel a lot, a hard case made of aluminum or molded plastic is a better choice. On hard cases, the weak points generally are the latches and hinge. Make sure a case has strong, locking latches and a durable hinge. Molded-in bumpers help strengthen

plastic models. For occasional trips, a single case will do, but for serious traveling, consider a double bow case. Not only can you include a backup bow, but you can stuff a lot of clothes into it, too.

Consider using an unpadded cloth case when carrying your bow to and from a tree stand. The cloth case will protect your bow when you are walking through thick brush, and it meets the legal requirements in states that require you to case your bow before and after shooting hours. Once on stand, the case can be rolled up and stuffed in a fanny pack.

Targets

Bales of straw, compressed cardboard or cedar still work fine as archery targets, but commercial targets last longer and are easier to use than the old standbys.

Indian cord-grass backstops, long used for archery tournaments, also make good home targets. "Beanbag" targets consist of a burlap or similar cover filled with cotton batting, shredded nylon or other materials. Beanbags have an excellent life expectancy, can be used nearly anywhere and arrows can be pulled easily from them. Laminated foam targets also are convenient to use. Small polyethylene foam targets are excellent for checking bowsights in camp, though you may have trouble pulling arrows from them.

Thanks to the growing popularity of 3-D tournaments, 3-D animal targets have become popular with hunters as well as target archers. These targets let you tune your skills on realistic animal targets before the hunt. Most animal targets hold up well to thousands of shots with field points.

Taking the concept of "live" target practice one step further, interactive video systems project animals onto a screen. From a distance of 20 yards, you shoot at these animals with special blunt arrows. The system is surprisingly realistic and provides excellent practice for hunting situations. Many big archery shops have installed these video systems.

The perfect broadhead target has not yet been invented, because sharp broadheads shred most materials. Laminated foam targets, which consist of rigid front and back layers and softer core layers to allow for easy broadhead removal, work about as well as any. Many of these have replaceable aiming dots; once you've shot out a dot, you punch it out of the target and insert a new core.

Many 3-D targets with pliable outer layers and dense foam cores make good broadhead targets, although it can be difficult to remove arrows. It's common for shooters to pull the head off the arrow shaft when removing an arrow from a 3-D. Most 3-D targets have replaceable cores or center sections; when the target gets shredded, you can replace just one section rather than the whole target. Or, you can fill in the damaged section with a foam repair kit.

In setting up an archery range, safety always comes first. Never shoot toward a neighbor's house, and don't expect a flimsy wood fence to stop an errant arrow. Set up your target in front of a brick wall or dirt bank, or shoot toward an open field. Or, place your target inside your garage and shoot from the driveway into the garage.

POPULAR TARGETS include: (1) beanbag, (2) laminated foam, (3) hay bales, (4) 3-D target and (5) blunt target.

Bowfishing Equipment

Reels

For bowfishing, the bow is equipped with a reel filled with fishing line. Several types of reels are used in bowfishing, but the most popular are drum-type and retriever styles. With a drum-type reel, the archer retrieves the arrow after the shot by wrapping the line around the drum by hand. Retriever-style reels utilize a handle system similar to a conventional fishing reel. Standard close-faced spinning reels are also used for bowfishing. The reels are usually attached to the bow using the stabilizer bushing.

Dacron line is preferred for bowfishing, because the line is limp and will not tangle as easily as heavy monofilament. Use 30- to 80-lb. test line, depending on the size of the fish you're after.

Bowfishing is very popular with some archers, in large part because it provides off-season shooting practice. With long seasons and the wide availability of rough fish, such as carp and gar, you can bowfish for much of the year throughout North America. Some special equipment is required to take fish with a bow.

Bows

Nearly any bow can be adapted for bowfishing, though recurves and compound bows are the most popular. Recurves are light in weight, quick to shoot and have few moving parts to tangle the string. Compound bows, especially those with light draw weights, are preferred by many bowfishermen, because compounds can be held at full draw while you wait for a fish to show itself.

Arrows

Arrows used for bowfishing must be heavy, because they must penetrate the water as well as the fish. Solid fiberglass, aluminum (below) or laminated arrows are the most common choice, because they are both heavy and durable. Fletchings, when used, should be made of rubber to withstand constant soakings. Many arrows have no fletching at all, since the trailing string stablizes the arrow sufficiently.

Fish arrows have holes drilled at the head and the nock ends for attaching line and can be rigged in different fashions using these holes. You can tie the line to the head end, to the nock end, or to the head end and then through the nock end and on to the reel.

Another method uses a separate heavy monofiliment line or light steel cable that is attached only to the two holes. One end of a barrel

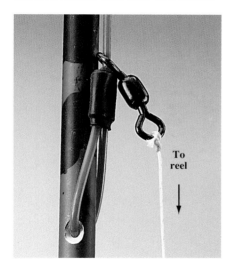

To
reel

swivel is attached to this line, then the line from the reel is attached to the other end of the barrel swivel (above). This method reduces tangles when the arrow is shot.

Arrowheads

Bowfishing heads are barbed so that they will penetrate and not pull out when you are fighting the fish in. Removal of the arrow is accomplished in different ways, depending on the design of the head.

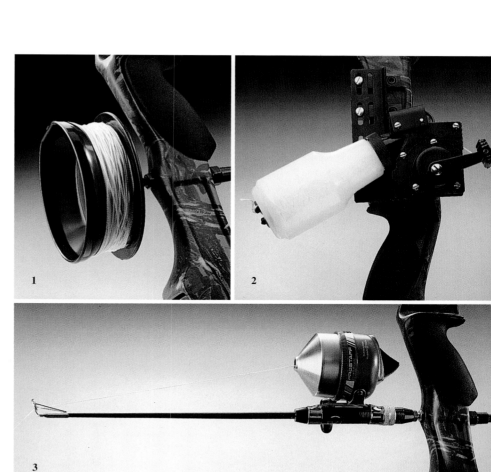

BOWFISHING REELS include: (1) conventional drum reels, (2) enclosed retriever reels and (3) closed-faced spinning reels.

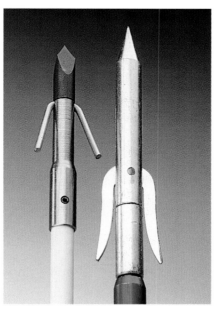

HEADS for bowfishing are barbed so they go through the fish but won't pull out. To simplify removal from the fish, the heads are designed so the barbs can either be reversed in direction, or removed from the head entirely.

ROLLER ARROW RESTS are often used when bowfishing to support the weight of the heavy arrow.

Bowhunting Skills

CORRECT SHOOTING FORM requires proper body position, a good stance and correct hand positions. In other shooting positions, such as a kneeling posture (inset), the same principles apply.

Shooting & Practice

Accurate, consistent shooting with a compound bow requires good mechanics honed by specific practice techniques, but mental conditioning and state of mind are equally important. (See pp. 96-101 for information on shooting with a traditional bow.)

If there is a key secret to good shooting, it is to relax, get out of the way and let the bow shoot the arrow. If you try to force a bow to perform in a particular way, or try to force an arrow into the target, you create muscle tension that makes it nearly impossible to duplicate the same form shot after shot. But if you learn to relax, your body will assume the same natural position each shot, and the result will be consistent accuracy.

A relaxed shooting form also cuts down on fatigue and muscle soreness and allows you to shoot for longer periods of time and with less chance of injury. Most archery coaches and top shooters agree that relaxation is the very foundation for all good shooting. You can see evidence of this by watching videos or looking at photos of the best archers in action. A top-notch archer is utterly relaxed – no tensed jaw, no squinted eyes, no clenched hands. While holding at full draw, expert shooters look almost drowsy.

Proper warm-up is essential to preventing overuse injuries, such as tendonitis and bursitis. Before drawing your bow, do some arm circles, shoulder shrugs, isometrics and stretching exercises to warm up your arm, shoulder and back muscles. If you shoot a bow with reasonable draw weight and warm up for a few minutes before each shooting session, you may save yourself years of arm, shoulder and back pain.

Mechanics of Shooting

STANCE. A research project before the 1984 Olympics showed that leg strength was the single most important variable in predicting high tournament archery scores. If your upper body is swaying like a weed in the wind, your sights will be swaying too, and strong legs are what hold your upper body – and your sights – steady during a shot.

Strong legs are a starting point, but the stance itself can also affect your shooting. The Olympic study found that an archer can reduce sway and hold more steadily on target by making minor adjustments in stance.

Begin by standing with your feet spread apart at shoulder width, 90 degrees to the target. Then take a half-step back with the front foot and pivot slightly toward the target for a mildly open stance. Keep your weight evenly distributed on both feet, and stand straight up, with your head directly over the center of your body. Maintain this stance as you raise the bow to shoot. Don't lean forward or backward to pull the bow, and don't cock your head to the side to line up your sights.

Obviously, a perfect stance isn't always possible in hunting situations, but you can apply the same principles. In a tree stand, either assume a solid sitting position, or stand with the same posture described above. When you're forced to squat or kneel on the ground to shoot, position yourself for good upper body stability. If you're kneeling, plant both knees solidly on the ground rather than kneeling on one knee and extending the other. Practice different

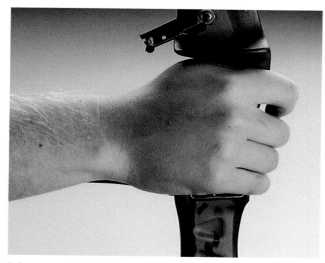

LOW-WRIST POSITION places the meaty part of the thumb on the bow handle. Maximum pressure falls about 1 inch below the big joint of the thumb. In this position, the wrist is more stable and less likely to move side to side.

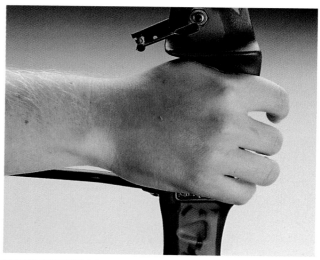

HIGH-WRIST POSITION minimizes hand contact with the bow but makes it difficult to avoid side-to-side wrist movement. Even slight wrist movement at the bow can lead to a substantial miss at the target.

postures to learn which are most stable under various field situations.

BOW HAND. Slight variations in hand placement can greatly affect arrow flight. This can be demonstrated by shooting arrows through paper at the target range, a common tuning technique. Altering hand placement between shots will change the angle at which the arrow hits the paper, which will affect the sizes of your arrow groups. For tight groups and consistent accuracy, you must place your hand on the bow identically for every shot.

Consistent hand position is easiest to achieve with a grip that minimizes hand-to-bow contact – a grip generally called a *low-wrist* position. To achieve this natural position, hold your hand out at arm's length, as if pointing at a distant mountain, and notice that your hand is not held vertically but is tilted to the side. Keeping your hand in this natural, tilted position, place the bow handle into your hand. You should feel pressure from the bow handle only on the meaty part of your thumb. Avoid palming the bow, which creates two pressure points – the thumb and the heel of the hand. With your hand in that relaxed position, your little finger will not hang in front of the bow handle, but to the side.

As you draw the bow, your hand should stay totally relaxed, with fingers that hang loosely throughout the shot. Some archers extend their fingers stiffly or choke the bow handle. Such finger positions indicate tension in the hand and arm, which can torque the bow and decrease accuracy.

STRING HAND. Like the bow hand, the drawing hand should remain in a naturally rotated position

throughout the shot. To ensure such a position, it's best to use a release aid with a rotating head that won't torque the string as you draw. With a wrist-strap release, you should feel a pull only on the strap, and your fingers should remain loose throughout the shot. With a finger-held release, your wrist should stay straight and relaxed.

If you release with your fingers, start by grasping the string at the first joints of your first three fingers, with the index finger above the arrow nock, the other two fingers below the nock. Like the bow hand, the string hand should be rotated slightly in a natural position. If you try to hold your hand absolutely vertical, your hand will try to rotate back to a naturally rotated position as you draw, torquing the string and producing a rough release. As you draw, the middle finger should hold most of the weight, and the other two fingers should float on the string. Some experienced shooters drop the index finger off the string at full draw to lessen finger contact with the string.

THE DRAW. With a solid stance and hands placed correctly on the bow and string, you're ready to draw and aim. Hold the bow at arm's length, roughly aiming at the target and begin to draw, pulling only with the muscles of your back. Your arm is merely the link between the bowstring and your back, and your wrist, forearm and biceps should stay relaxed even at full draw.

As you draw, don't change your stance or tip your head one way or the other to see through the peep. If you find it necessary to crane your neck, it means that your draw length is too long or short, or that your peep sight is in the wrong spot. Your bow

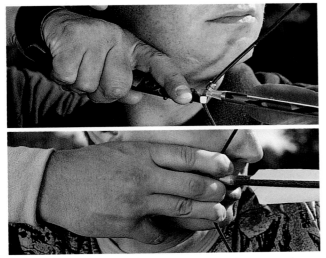

TYPICAL ANCHOR POINTS: With a wrist-strap release aid, many archers anchor with the big knuckle behind the jaw (top). With a finger-release, most archers anchor so the tip of the index or middle finger is at the corner of the mouth.

should be set up so the draw is as smooth and relaxed as possible. Don't conform to your bow; make your bow conform to you.

And don't hunch your shoulder (a common problem when shooting too much draw weight), because this means you are holding the bow arm in line with your shoulder muscles. To ensure a solid bow arm, pull your shoulder low so the arm bone presses directly into your shoulder, bone to bone.

When you reach the valley – the point at which a compound bow let-off reaches its lowest draw weight – anchor solidly and aim at the target.

ANCHOR. No one can prescribe a best way to anchor with a release aid. With a wrist-strap release, many archers anchor with the big knuckle of the index finger pressed behind the jaw. With a finger-held release, experienced shooters commonly anchor with the back of the hand pressed against the jaw. More important than the precise method is consistency. You must anchor solidly and identically every shot.

Finger-release shooters typically use one of two anchoring points. Most hunters anchor fairly high, with the tip of the index finger planted solidly in the corner of the mouth. Tournament archers generally use a lower anchor point, with the string hand under the chin. To anchor solidly, they press the big knuckle of the thumb behind the chin bone.

RELEASE. Whether you shoot using sights or shoot barebow, with release aids or with your fingers, the critical moment of releasing the bowstring should be marked by complete relaxation. As you hold at full draw, calm your mind and body and let your sight

drift naturally across the target. Don't tense up in an attempt to hold the sight in the center of the target; let the bow travel through its natural arc of movement.

To achieve this kind of relaxation, the moment of release should come as a surprise. If you're using a release aid, shooting a bow is similar to firing a rifle, where you aim, relax and slowly squeeze the trigger until the gun surprises you by going off.

To ensure this element of surprise, you must avoid thinking about the release. Forget about the string, and focus only on pulling with your back muscles; as you increase pressure with your back – some archers call this "increasing back tension" – your hand will slowly tighten and trigger the release.

With the bow hand completely relaxed at the moment of release, some hunters worry about dropping the bow. If you find yourself anticipating the shot and unconsciously gripping the handle to keep your bow from slipping, equip your bow with a wrist sling. With a sling, you can keep your bow hand relaxed, even after you've released the string, without fear of dropping an expensive bow.

Finger-release shooters should also strive for relaxation at the moment of release. The release is a matter of relaxing your fingers and allowing the string to slip away. Never throw open your hand; instead, concentrate on lifting your elbow up and back, pulling with your back and allowing your string fingers to relax. As one professional instructor said, "Don't let go of the string. Let the string go. There's a big difference."

With a relaxed release, your hand will move straight back, near to your face, and your fingers should be limp and relaxed. If your fingers are stiff, you've opened your hand deliberately to get rid of the string. If your hand moves out to the side of your face, you plucked the string. If it moves forward, it has followed the string. Make sure your hand always moves back along your face and your fingers are relaxed.

FOLLOW-THROUGH. As the arrow leaves the bow, your hands and arms should hold the same position and your bow should move very little. The shot itself is simply a brief interruption in the act of aiming. Once your arrow has hit the target, then you can lower the bow to see where it has hit.

If the bow jerks violently down or to the side, there is tension somewhere in your form. Try adjusting your alignment by opening or closing your stance, and work on your bow hand, bow arm and string hand to eliminate tension that could be torquing the bow or throwing it to the side.

Practice shooting close distances with eyes closed (inset) and shooting long distances

Practice Techniques

As you practice your stance, draw, release and follow-through, shoot each arrow as though it's the only arrow you'll shoot that day. Building good form is the result of practice quality, not quantity. It's better to shoot 10 good arrows than 100 bad ones that do nothing but ingrain bad habits. If you do make a bad shot, analyze it briefly to determine the problem, then forget about it and go on. Always keep a positive attitude; if fatigue sets in and you begin to lose control, quit for the day and wait until you're fresh and enthusiastic to begin a new practice session.

Three basic training techniques can help improve your form rapidly and are especially useful for beginning archers.

First, shoot with your eyes closed (above). Stand 10 feet or so from the backdrop so you don't miss the target, then mentally inspect your bow arm, shooting arm and stance as you execute a shot. Focus on relaxing, pulling with your back and squeezing the release slowly (or relaxing your fingers). After the bow goes off, follow through, and before opening your eyes, again run through the checkpoints. Are you still on target? Are your hands relaxed?

As you're first learning, shoot this way regularly to develop and ingrain good shooting habits. And once you become an experienced archer, warm up before each practice session with some closed-eye shooting to get the feel of a good shot.

A second practice technique is to remove the sight from your bow and shoot at a blank target with no aiming spot. This routine allows you to forget about where your arrows are hitting and concentrate solely on form.

A final technique is to shoot at long distances – 60 to 80 yards or so – a practice that helps build good follow-through. At release, resist the urge to drop your bow arm to watch the arrow, and hold your sights on the target until the arrow hits. Ingraining this kind of follow-through will improve your accuracy at any distance.

Along with these form-building techniques, practice regularly shooting at targets to develop your accuracy. If you can't hit an inanimate target under good conditions, you have little chance of making clean hits on game animals, either. Practice until you can shoot your arrows within a 2-inch group at 20 yards, 3-inch at 30, 4-inch at 40, 5-inch at 50. This precision accuracy will serve you well later in hunting.

Once you develop good form and precision accuracy, the systematic drills described below will help you adapt your skills for field shooting. If you practice these drills until they become automatic and second nature to you, you'll be well on your way to becoming a successful hunting archer.

SHOOT SLOW. The movement of drawing the bow may be the most significant limitation in bowhunting, because motion alerts close-range animals. But if you can draw so slowly that an animal fails to see the movement, even when looking your way, you'll rarely lose a shot opportunity.

With the herky-jerky draw cycle of a compound bow, developing a motionless draw isn't easy. To perfect it, hold your bow in shooting position, aim and draw as slowly as possible. Your sights should hold steady on target, and your string hand should come back steadily with no jerks or pauses. Do this six to ten times per session, building up to a full 10 seconds per draw. If you find it impossible to draw your bow straight back, the draw weight is too heavy.

SHOOT FAST. At other times, you must be able to draw and shoot quickly. Shooting quickly comes easiest for instinctive shooters armed with longbows or recurves, but with practice, a compound-bow hunter using sights can learn to shoot quickly. To develop efficiency, see how many arrows you can shoot in a 1-minute period. Then see how quickly you can extract and shoot all of the arrows from your quiver. These are great drills for shooting efficiency. But remember, all shots must be accurate; wild shots mean nothing.

Shoot in bad weather

SHOOT IN BAD WEATHER. If you practice only under good conditions, you'll be ready only for good conditions. To prepare for realistic hunting conditions, practice in wind, rain and snow. Not only will you learn how to shoot in adverse conditions, but you'll also learn how your tackle performs. In snow, you might find that your arrow rest ices up; in rain, you might find that water plugs up your peep sight or makes your cable slide squeak. Only by shooting in actual hunting conditions can you analyze and correct subtle problems.

SHOOT IN ALL POSITIONS. When hunting in the field, it won't always be possible to shoot from an ideal stance. You may have to shoot around trees, under limbs, straight up hills or down into ravines. Systematic practice prepares you for all contingencies. Practice shooting while kneeling, sitting, leaning to the side, and at steep angles up and down. If you find that you simply can't shoot accurately from

Shoot in awkward positions

some positions, you've learned a valuable lesson: eliminate these postures and develop positions that work for you.

Once you've developed proficiency at several shooting positions, go into the field and practice assuming and shooting quickly from these positions. For more challenge, train by running through woods or climbing slopes between shots. This is especially good practice for mountain hunting where physical exertion can affect your accuracy.

SHOOT 3-D TARGETS. Prepare yourself for the pressure of hunting in the field. Participate in trail shoots and 3-D tournaments where you shoot at animal targets, not dots.

PRACTICE IN THE FIELD. "Stump-shooting" may be the most valuable practice of all. Whenever possible, roam through the woods and fields and shoot at rotten stumps, dirt clods and grass clumps. Stump-shooting is especially good for practicing while on hunting trips. Carry at least one practice arrow tipped with a rubber blunt or judo point, and any time you walk a trail or stop for lunch, shoot a few practice shots to keep yourself sharp for the real thing.

Stump shooting

Shooting with Sights

Although the general mechanics of shooting with sights are the same as those used for instinctive "barebow" shooting, there are specific aiming techniques unique to shooting a bow equipped with sights. In addition, you'll need to learn methods for sighting in your bow to ensure that your sights are adjusted accurately.

Setting a Peep Sight

Not all hunters use peep sights, but if you do, the peep must be set correctly before you can sight in the bow.

Inserting a peep into the string is a simple process of separating the strands of the bowstring and positioning the peep so the strings are divided evenly on both sides of the peep (opposite page). This job is easiest if you use a bow press to relieve tension on the string, but you can also separate the strands of the string using a dull screwdriver or other blunt object that won't fray the string. Some companies make special peep-inserting devices.

It is critical that the peep is lined up perfectly with your eye at full draw, so you don't have to tilt your head to look through it. One good test is to draw your bow with closed eyes, then open your eyes. You should be looking directly through the peep.

When your peep is set, add serving above and below the peep to hold it in place. Measure the distance from the peep to the nocking point for future reference; additional strings should all be set up the same way. (Note: If you shoot bows of different axle-to-axle lengths, the measurement from nocking point to peep will differ.)

Self-aligning peeps have a rubber tube that straightens the peep during the draw, but if you use a free-floating peep, you must set it so the string rotation places the peep in a straight position at full draw. In most cases, a free-floating peep rotates 45° to 90° during the draw, depending on the number of twists in your string and your shooting style.

If you have a bow press, you can relax your bow, detach one end of the string, twist it a half turn, and reattach it. Draw the bow to check peep alignment. Continue this process until the peep comes back just right.

As an alternative to using a bow press, slide the lock knots away from the peep, lift up a couple of strands of the string from one side of the peep (use your thumbnail or a dull screwdriver) and transfer these to the other side of the peep. With this technique, you can rotate a peep to any position without using a bow press.

How to Set a Peep Sight

USE a bow press to relax the bow and relieve string tension. If you don't have a bow press, a dull screwdriver can be used to separate the string (inset).

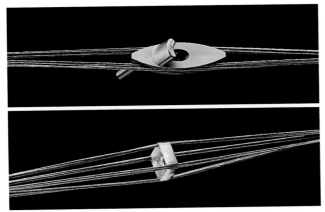

INSERT the peep into the string, with half the strands on each side of the peep (top). Some horizontally mounted peeps (bottom) have three or four string grooves; on these, divide the string so equal numbers of strands fit into each groove.

ADJUST the peep so it lines up with your eye at full draw. Make sure to maintain a natural shooting position, and anchor as you do when shooting, without tilting your head. As you hold at full draw, have a helper move the peep until it is directly in front of your eye.

How to Serve a Peep Sight

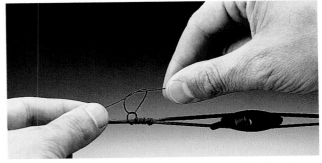

TIE a series of 10 granny knots around the string just above the peep, using braided serving thread. Alternate knots on each side of the string, and finish with a square knot.

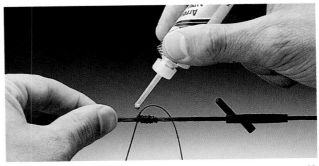

SECURE the square knot with a drop of glue, then cut off the loose ends.

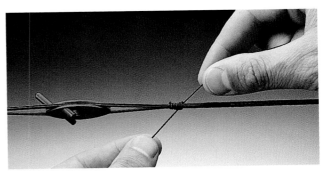

TIE a second series of knots just below the peep.

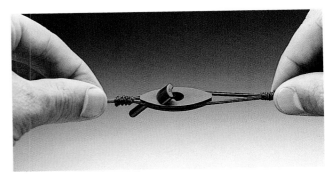

SLIDE the knotted servings tight against the top and bottom of the peep to hold it in place. If you need to move the peep, the servings can be slid away from the peep. Attach rubber tubing to the peep, if it is a self-aligning peep.

SHOOT arrow groups at the exact distance of the top sight pin to determine if the pin is correctly aligned. If the arrow groups (red marks) are off center, move the pin toward the point of impact. Shoot several arrow groups, adjusting the pin until the arrows hit where the pin is positioned.

Adjusting Pin Sights

With your peep sight in place, you can sight in your bow by adjusting the pin sights. If your bow sight uses four pins set at 10-yard intervals from 20 to 50 yards – the most common sight configuration – begin by shooting a three-arrow group from exactly 20 yards, using the top sight pin. If the arrows hit the center of the target, you can move on to the remaining pins. In most instances, however, you'll need to

adjust your top pin to bring the arrows on target.

Adjusting a sight pin is basically a matter of moving the pin so it aligns with the point of impact. In other words, if your arrows hit high, move the pin up; if the arrows hit left, move the pin left, and so forth. Continue to shoot arrow groups, moving the top sight pin until the arrows consistently hit where you're aiming.

When you have arrows hitting dead center at 20 yards, line all your sight pins up in a perfect vertical line. The easiest way to do this is by using the bowstring as a reference. Simply hold the bow at arm's length and look through the string as you adjust the pins so they are aligned with the string. To double-check the alignment, tape a card to the pins and visually line up the edge of this card with the string. With a cross-hair sight, of course, you would line up the vertical wire parallel with the bowstring.

With the 20-yard pin set and all the pins aligned vertically, measure off exactly 50 yards, and sight in your bottom pin using the same procedure. Once the 50-yard is set, position the 30- and 40-yard pins at even intervals between the top and bottom pins. With the pins evenly spaced, shoot several groups at each distance to fine-tune the settings, then tighten all the pins to lock them into place.

WHEN SIGHTED IN CORRECTLY, the pins on your sight will be aligned parallel to the string, with even intervals between the pins.

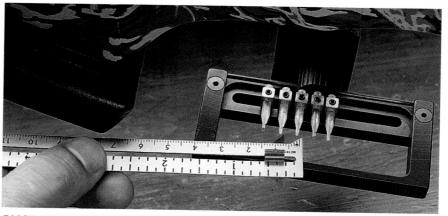

ONCE YOUR PIN SIGHT IS ADJUSTED, measure the pin interval for future reference. Any other bow with the same arrow speed will also have the same pin gap, so knowing the interval can help you roughly sight in a new bow.

Aiming with Sights

Despite the age-old advice to "pick a spot" on an animal when aiming a bow, many experts believe that shooters using sights are better off concentrating on the sight pin – or on a spot halfway between the pin and the target – not on the target itself.

The "pick-a-spot" approach resembles the technique used by shotgun hunters, where the shooter focuses directly on the target and sees the gun barrel only as a blur. This is the only approach available to instinctive bow shooters, since they have nothing but the target to focus on.

By contrast, a shooter armed with a pistol or rifle – or a bow equipped with sights – concentrates primarily on the sights and sees the target as a blur. Rather than concentrating on a specific spot, you're forming a visual picture with the sight superimposed over your target.

Many renowned authorities believe that focusing on the pins rather than the target is an inherently more accurate method of aiming. But focusing on the sight helps in another way, perhaps more psychological than mechanical. Under the tension of hunting, picking a spot on an animal takes enormous concentration. Using sights and focusing on the sight pins rather than the deer relieves the emotional pressure. Instead of looking at a live animal – a distant, emotion-stirring target – you are focused on a sight pin, a nearby, familiar, and nonemotional object. Transferring your attention from the animal and placing it on the sight pin makes you less susceptible to target panic.

THE ARC OF MOVEMENT. If you could hold your sight perfectly steady on a target, you'd hit the target with every shot. But all archers, even the most expert shooters, experience a certain amount of bow movement, known as an *arc of movement*. If you have an arc of movement of 3 inches at 20 yards, for example, you'll shoot within a 3-inch circle at 20 yards. The greater the distance, the greater the effect of this movement.

When striving for consistent accuracy, the goal is to reduce the arc of movement as much as possible. Beginners often try to achieve this by gritting their teeth and tensing their muscles, fighting to hold the bow absolutely steady, but this approach actually leads to worse shooting. The more tense you become while trying to hold dead center on the target, the worse your accuracy will be. If you have a natural arc of 3 inches, fighting the bow will cause your arrow groups to spread out to 4 or 5 inches.

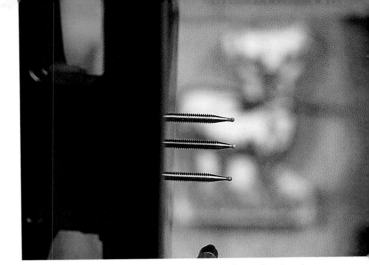

FOCUS on the sight pin, not a spot on the animal, when shooting with sights. For instinctive shooters, focusing on a spot on the animal is necessary, since there is no other focal point. But for shooters who use sights, focusing on the sight pin provides better accuracy and reduces target panic – a condition caused by the excitement of aiming at a live animal.

Ironically, the secret to reducing the arc of movement is to stop resisting it. You must learn to relax and let the bow move naturally, working with it rather than fighting it. Working to perfect your form and strengthen your muscles can obviously help improve your accuracy, but relaxation is the single most important element of accurate shooting.

How do you achieve this relaxed frame of mind? Imagine that you've drawn your bow and are aiming at your target. As your sight pin drifts back and forth across the center of the target, smoothly begin the release, either by slowly squeezing the trigger on your release aid or by gently relaxing your string fingers. Never try to stop your release or jerk the sight onto the target once you've started a shot. Once begun, the release process must continue smoothly without interruption. If you try to release too quickly, just as the sight pin covers the ideal target spot, you're almost certain to jerk or flinch – actions which are guaranteed to destroy accuracy.

Some people mistakenly think that shooting with sights is always a slow, analytical process. In reality, sight shooting is a deliberate and precise action, but it doesn't have to be slow. Once you learn to relax and stop fighting the movement of the bow, you may find that shooting with sights is faster and more accurate than shooting barebow.

Many hunters find that using larger sight pins helps them with accuracy. When you aim, large pins cover the target and reduce the perception of movement, while tiny pins appear to dance around wildly. When using large pins, look right at the pin instead of around it, and let the pin cover the target; your mind will automatically center it for you.

Estimating Range

Precisely adjusted sights and good aiming technique are essential to hunting success, but they won't count for much unless you also have the ability to estimate distances with fair accuracy. Imagine that you've got a trophy whitetail in your sights, with the 20-yard sight pin dead center in the animal's kill zone, and have just executed the perfect release. Every hunter's dream – unless your targeted deer is actually standing 30, not 20 yards away.

In some hunting situations, you can measure distances exactly. When hunting from a stand, for example, you can premeasure distances to nearby trees and rocks and use these objects as range indicators when animals approach. And in many stalking situations, you can use a rangefinder to gauge distances. If these methods are practical, use them; the more precisely you can measure range, the more precisely you can place your arrows.

In many instances, however, it is impossible to measure distances exactly and you must judge distances by eye alone. Some archers view range estimation as a cryptic art and give up trying to master it, but in reality, learning to judge distances is rather easy. The secret is to mentally divide long distances into small segments. If you practice regularly at 20 yards, for example, you can use this familiar distance as a reference for judging longer ranges.

Imagine that you're still-hunting through a forest and suddenly see a deer at an unknown distance. You

PREMEASURE DISTANCES to nearby reference points when hunting from a stand. Use this information to quickly judge distances when an animal approaches your position.

Using Rangefinders

Rangefinders allow you to estimate distances accurately, improving your chances for a clean shot. A rangefinder that measures distances from 10 to 60 yards is sufficient for a bowhunter. Rangefinders come in two basic styles. Optical rangefinders (1) are lightweight, inexpensive and fairly accurate. Laser rangefinders (2) are very precise and easy to use, but are expensive.

ESTIMATE LONG SHOTS by mentally dividing the distance into smaller, more familiar increments. Most hunters, for example, are familiar with the 20-yard distances commonly used on target ranges, and can use this knowledge to judge longer shots. Don't expect your estimates to be perfect; learning to gauge distances with an error of 5 yards or less is sufficient.

could simply look at the deer and guess at the range, based on your gut feeling or instincts, and occasionally you'll be close enough to make a killing shot. More often, though, you'll miss. First, the size of deer varies so greatly that it can be very difficult to estimate an animal's range. In addition, lighting, terrain and foliage all affect depth perception, and as these variables change, so will your distance perception.

For this reason, it's better to break the distance down into smaller increments, looking at the ground and other indicators rather than at the deer itself. Pick a spot 20 yards away – a distance you can judge easily based on target shooting experience. From this relatively sure reference, expand your estimate in 5-yard increments, silently saying something like, "If it's 20 yards to that tree, then it looks like another 5 yards to the bush, then another 5 yards to the rock, and another 5 yards to the deer. He's about 35 yards away."

Such a method might sound too time-consuming to be practical, but with experience it becomes second nature. And practicing the skill is easy. Whenever you're walking down the street or along a trail, pick out an object ahead, mentally estimate the range, then measure the distance by pacing it off. For most people, a relaxed walking step covers about 1 yard, but for best accuracy, you should measure your stride exactly.

Such practice will greatly increase your ability to estimate distances accurately. A military study showed experienced observers could consistently estimate to within 15 percent of actual measured distances, while untrained observers rarely did that well.

Visual range estimation has limitations and will never be as accurate as an optical or laser rangefinder. You'll never be perfect, so don't try. Instead, limit your estimates to the 5-yard increments. Trying to fine-tune an estimate, say to 33 or 38 yards, only wastes time and is not necessary. If you learn to estimate quickly and instinctively to within 5 yards of actual distances at ranges from 20 to 50 yards, you'll have all the accuracy you need for bowhunting. For any game closer than 20 yards, you essentially can aim dead on with your 20-yard pin, because a reasonably fast arrow will hit only a couple of inches high at 10 to 15 yards – well within the kill zone on a deer.

Remember one last point, however. Given the potential for 15 percent ranging error, your effective range has definite limits. At 40 yards, for example, a 15 percent ranging error would be plus or minus 6 yards. An extremely fast bow will hit the kill zone with such an error level, but beyond 40 yards, it will not. So 40 yards marks a practical limitation on estimating distances by eye. For shots farther than that, a conscientious bowhunter either will use a rangefinder or will pass up the shot.

TRAJECTORY refers to the curved path (dashed line) an arrow follows from bow to target.

Understanding Arrow Trajectory

The slower the speed of a projectile, the more it will drop over the course of its flight. To compensate for this drop, a projectile must be fired in an arched path to successfully strike the intended target. The arrow starts below the archer's line of sight, rises above it, and then drops back to his line of sight at the target. This curve in an arrow's path between bow and target is known as *trajectory*.

Trajectory is a crucial concern in bowhunting because a bowhunter simply can't escape its effects. People who contend that modern bows are so fast they're almost like rifles simply don't understand trajectory. Trajectory is directly related to the speed of a projectile, and the very fastest bows shoot about 300 feet per second (fps) compared to the fast rifle at 3,000 fps. An arrow fired from such a bow has a greater trajectory over 30 yards than does a rifle bullet over 300 yards.

Instinctive shooters who must visualize the path of their arrows to the target know the importance of trajectory. But sight shooters with an understanding of trajectory find it easier to make good sight settings and are better able to avoid branches and other obstacles. And to accurately shoot uphill and downhill, an understanding of trajectory is essential.

Visualizing Trajectory

Hitting obstacles ranks as one of the major reasons for missed shots, especially for hunters pursuing whitetail deer and other forest animals. A clear understanding of trajectory can help you prevent many of these misses.

First, remember that an arrow starts below your line of sight – as much as 6 inches or more if you're a release-aid shooter with a low anchor point. When your line of sight is well above an obstacle, there is a tendency to assume the arrow will clear with no problem. But because the arrow remains below your line of sight until it is 4 to 5 yards away from the bow, it can slam into a nearby obstacle if you don't elevate high enough. Many hunters have blown easy shots by hitting stumps, rocks and other objects directly in front of them.

Learn to visualize arrow trajectory so you can cleanly shoot under or over limbs and other obstacles. It's possible, of course, to compute trajectory mathematically, but it's not necessarily practical and may not help you in the field. Some simple steps on the target range will help you actually see the trajectory of your arrows.

Make sure your bow is sighted in at regular intervals, such as 20, 30, 40 and 50 yards. To determine the trajectory of your arrows at the halfway mark, you'll be shooting target groups for each sight pin from a distance equal to half their sighted distance. First, stand 10 yards from the target and aim at the bullseye with your 20-yard pin. Shoot several groups, measuring the distance of each arrow above the center of the target; then average these numbers. This average is your midrange trajectory at 20 yards.

Shoot additional groups at 15 yards with your 30-yard pin; 20 yards with your 40-yard pin; 25 yards with your 50-yard pin. With increasing distance, you'll find that your arrows hit progressively higher, giving you a clear picture of the trajectory at each distance. For a bow shooting about 220 feet per second (fps), the midrange trajectory at 20 yards will be roughly 3 inches; at 30 yards, 6 inches; at 40 yards, 12 inches; and at 50 yards, 20 inches. At higher arrow speeds, the trajectory will be less; at slower speeds, greater. This method doesn't give peak trajectories,

away using your 30-yard pin. But your 20-yard pin falls on a limb about 20 yards away. Your shot will miss the deer, and the arrow will hit the limb.

Sight Window

At any given distance, you have some leeway when estimating range, and this leeway is called a *sight window*. Understanding the sight windows for your bow can help with shot selection. Again, the best way to learn about sight windows is by thorough practice-range work.

To gauge the window for your 20-yard sight pin, for example, shoot at an 8-inch target, which is roughly the size of a large deer's kill zone when it is standing broadside. Start at 20 yards, and move closer, 1 yard at a time, always aiming at the center of the target with your 20-yard pin. The arrows will gradually move up until they begin hitting above the 8-inch target. That's the minimum end of your sight window. Now start again at 20 yards, and move back,

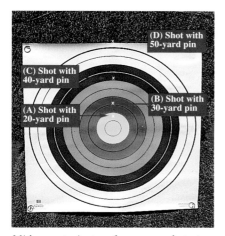

Midrange trajectory for arrows shot at (A) 10 yards = 3" above center, (B) 15 yards = 6" above center, (C) 20 yards = 12" above center and (D) 25 yards = 20" above center

which are slightly closer to the target, but it does give you a practical picture of midrange trajectory.

How do you put this knowledge to practical use? Let's assume you've drawn a bead on a buck standing 30 yards away, and there is a tree limb hanging in your path 15 yards out, directly in the sight path between your bowsight and the deer's chest. An archer with no knowledge of trajectory might believe he has to maneuver to shoot either above and below the branch, but from your range test experience, you know that your arrow will be 6 inches above your line of sight at the midway point in its flight. Fire away; your arrow will clear the branch cleanly. Similarly, if the offending branch is 6 inches or so above the sight line, many hunters would shoot, unaware that the arrow is likely to strike the branch. You, however, will seek a new shooting position, looking for a sight line which ensures that the arrow's midpoint trajectory is a safe distance away from the tree branch.

Remember also that when a sight pin rests on an object at the same distance as the sighted distance of the pin, the arrow will likely hit the object. Imagine, for example, that you've put a pin on a deer 30 yards

DETERMINE SIGHT WINDOWS for each of your sight pins. The archer shown here is finding the sight window for the 20-yard pin. In this case, the sight window was 8 yards – from 16 to 24 yards.

1 yard at a time, until your arrows hit below the circle. That's the maximum end of your sight window.

Repeat this test for each sight pin; for the 30-yard pin, start at 30 yards; for the 40-yard pin, start at 40 yards; and so forth. Move from the starting point toward the minimum end of each sight window; then move back from the starting point to determine the maximum end. The sight windows will become proportionately shorter as you move to the pins sighted for longer distances, due to the increasing arc of the trajectory.

Shooting on an Angle

Bows are generally sighted in for horizontal shots, where arrow trajectories are predictable. However, when you shoot from a high tree stand or on an uphill or downhill slope, the rules for trajectory change.

At a given distance, gravity has the greatest effect on trajectory for an arrow flying horizontally, and has gradually less effect as the shooting angle is raised or lowered. The reason for this is that the trajectory arc is determined by the horizontal distance the arrow travels, not the overall distance. When shooting at steep angles, either up or down, aiming for the actual distance to the target is a mistake, since this measurement may be considerably larger than the horizontal distance that governs the arrow's trajectory. For example, if you shoot at a target 40 yards away down a steep hill, using your 40-yard sight pin, your shot will probably go high of the mark (opposite page). At steep angles, you must learn to compensate by aiming low.

Contrary to common opinion, this principle applies equally to uphill and downhill shots. It's true that uphill trajectory begins to differ from downhill trajectory at some point, because gravity slows an arrow flying up faster than one flying down. But within standard hunting distances – 50 yards and less – the difference is not significant. For practical purposes, then, slant range can be computed identically, whether the slope is uphill or down.

The trick, of course, is determining how low to aim at different distances and slope angles. You can calculate this information geometrically (opposite page), but to do so requires a calculator, electronic rangefinder, clinometer for measuring the angle of slopes and a good head for mathematics.

If you choose the mathematical method, you can simplify this work by using a chart like the example shown here (right). A complete chart for all practical shooting distances will help you make clean kills at steep angles. To put such a chart to practical use, however, you must know the distance to the target and angle of slope. Steep slopes make range estima-

Sample Trajectory Adjustment Chart

Angle of slope in degrees (up or down)	Divide estimated range by this number	Sight picture (40 yards actual distance)
10	1.02	39
15	1.04	38.5
20	1.06	38
25	1.10	36.5
30	1.15	35
35	1.22	33
40	1.31	30.5
45	1.41	28

Charts such as this one, taken from The Complete Book of Rifles and Shotguns *by Jack O'Connor, can help you calculate trajectory changes when shooting on an incline*

tion difficult at best, so a good rangefinder can help here. With practice you can learn to estimate slope visually, or you can buy a compass with a built-in clinometer to measure slope. Or, you can buy an expensive forester's clinometer, which measures angle of slope precisely.

To be honest, using mathematics to calculate shooting adjustments is not very practical for most hunters. In the field, game animals rarely give you enough time to make the measurements and computations, and few hunters are enthused by the prospect of carrying a rangefinder, calculator and printed charts into the field.

Most shooters find that simple practice gives them a feel for how upward and downward angles affect arrow trajectory. You can practice by shooting from a tree stand set to different heights, for example. At each height, shoot several groups at varying distances from your stand.

Reducing Trajectory

Flattening the trajectory of an arrow reduces the need for precise range estimation, streamlines the process for shooting over and under obstacles and simplifies adjustments needed when shooting at upward and downward angles. Several factors – fletching style, arrow weight and air density – can affect trajectory, but arrow speed has the single greatest influence. For

Effects of Slope on Trajectory

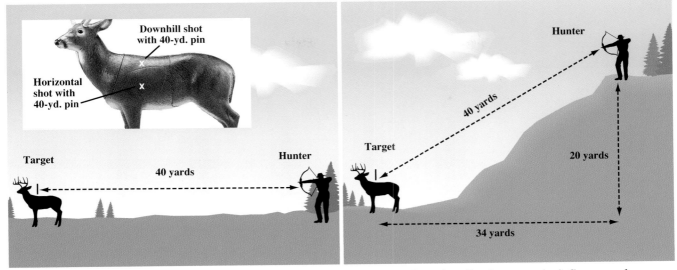

THE EFFECTS OF SLOPE on trajectory can be explained by the physics of gravity. Gravity exerts its influence only against the horizontal distance of an arrow's flight. When you shoot horizontally at a target 40 yards away (left), gravity exerts its influence for a full 40 yards, and the arrow's drop follows expectations. But when you shoot downhill (right) or uphill at a target 40 yards away, the horizontal distance can actually be much less, as shown above. In this situation, if you shoot using the 40-yard sight pin, your arrow will hit high on the target (inset), since it has not had time to complete its normal trajectory drop for 40 horizontal yards.

this reason, manufacturers and archers continually seek ways to make their bows faster and faster.

You can increase arrow speed in several ways. One method is to reduce arrow weight. Each 5-grain reduction in arrow weight provides a speed increase of about 1 foot per second (fps). Thus, if you reduce arrow weight by 100 grains, you increase speed by roughly 20 fps.

Arrow speed can also be gained by increasing the draw weight of the bow. A 1-pound increase in draw weight yields an increase of about 2 fps in speed. Thus if you crank draw weight up by 10 pounds, you gain 20 fps in arrow speed.

Finally, shooting a bow with harder cams can increase speed. At a given draw weight, hard cams can provide 10 to 20 percent more speed than round wheels.

Up to a point, speed is good. But remember that the faster the arrow, the more "critically" it shoots. That is, faster arrows are more susceptible to uncontrolled oscillations and are more difficult to shoot with accuracy. At some point, the loss in accuracy and consistency that comes with ultrafast arrows may negate any gains you get from the flattened trajectory. Faster arrows also make it harder to tune the bow, especially when the arrows are equipped with broadheads.

Remember, accuracy is the number-one ingredient in clean kills. Lightning-fast arrows do you no good if they don't consistently hit the target.

Using Geometry to Calculate Arrow Trajectory

Here's how geometry can be used to calculate how arrow trajectory changes when shooting on an incline:

Visualize the hunting situation as a right-angle triangle, with two perpendicular legs; (A), the distance from the hunter to the ground; and (B), the distance from the animal to the ground directly below the hunter. The sloped hypotenuse, (C), is the distance from the hunter to the animal. In essence, the drop of an arrow fired along the inclined hypotenuse will equal the drop of an arrow traveling the horizontal distance (B).

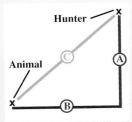

For example, imagine you're on a cliff, where you spot a buck standing below at a 45-degree angle to your line of sight. Your rangefinder shows that the distance along the sloped line to the buck is 30 yards. Using a basic formula from geometry, called the Pythagorean Theorem ($A^2 + B^2 = C^2$), you can calculate that side B, representing the horizontal distance to the deer, is roughly 21 yards. To hit the deer in the kill zone, then, you would use the 20-yard sight pin, not the 30-yard pin.

Instinctive Shooting

Instinctive shooting is the art of shooting a bow without the assistance of any kind of aiming device or release aid. The arrow is not used for reference, nor is any part of the bow used for sighting purposes. The shooter simply concentrates his vision on the spot he wishes to hit, and the brain unconsciously directs the hands and eyes to point the arrow correctly. The process is much like that of throwing a ball or casting a fishing lure – you focus only on the target, and the brain instinctively coordinates hand and arm movement to achieve the goal.

Instinctive shooting is the least complicated and most basic method of aiming a bow and has a long history. English longbowmen aimed their arrows instinctively at Crecy and Agincourt, as did their predecessors, the feared bow horsemen of Asia, the Mongols and the Huns. For a century and a half, the Native American Indian used his instinctive shooting ability to feed, clothe and protect his family.

Prior to the advent of the compound bow in the 1970s, most hunting bows were aimed and shot by the instinctive method. With the compound bow, however, came a different approach to aiming. Because its mechanical let-off made it possible for an archer to hold at full draw for extended periods, the compound bow lent itself well to sights and various aiming accoutrements. Within a few years, instinctive shooting all but disappeared as archers enthusiastically adopted sophisticated sighting systems.

Today, however, with the resurgence and growing popularity of the recurve and longbow, instinctive shooting has resurfaced as a favored technique for hunting bows. Historically, the recurve and longbow were aimed and shot instinctively, so it is natural that many devotees of this equipment wish to shoot in the same manner. And in practical terms, instinctive shooting is well matched to traditional equipment; recurves and longbows increase in poundage as they are drawn, and can be difficult to shoot using complicated aiming systems that require the shooter to remain at full draw for several seconds.

Archers using traditional recurves and longbows are the most likely candidates for instinctive shooting, but the skill is gaining favor among compound bow shooters, as well. The instinctive shooter can draw and shoot quicker than one using a sighting system, and the style also allows more versatility when hunting in tight spots calling for quick decisions. For competitive shooting, few archers would argue that the bowsight is more accurate than instinctive shooting, but hunters who become adept at the style are convinced that instinctive shooting is the best method.

Basics

Instinctive shooting is easily learned, but it is not an inherent skill. Like throwing a ball, instinctive shooting is a skill honed by experience and practice. A child learning to throw a ball gradually learns how to change the arc of the ball when throwing to different distances. He learns this by repeatedly watching the ball in flight. Likewise, an instinctive shooter perfects his accuracy by watching countless arrows in flight.

Because instinctive shooting uses no bowsight or other physical aiming device, it is crucial that the shooter have a clear understanding of the process. Without this knowledge, a shooter has little chance of analyzing his shots or improving his skills.

Instinctive shooting utilizes basic hand-eye coordination skills. In effect, the bow hand serves as the front sight, and the eye serves as the rear sight. Although we talk about pointing the arrow, in actuality, we are pointing the bow hand where the eye is looking. The arrow happens to lie along the line between the hand and eye, but it has no bearing on the actual aiming process.

ARROW POSITION. It is crucial that the arrow be as close as possible to the line between the eye and the bow hand. For this reason, instinctive shooters generally shoot "off the shelf" with no arrow rest. This puts the arrow as close as possible to the bow hand. When shot off the shelf, the arrow becomes an extension of the pointing hand and is an integral part of the hand/eye coordination effort.

Relationship of arrow to the hand

STANCE. Begin by standing 90° to the target, with your feet at shoulder width. Move your left foot (for a right-handed archer) back about 1/2 step (below), and turn your body and feet about 1/4 turn toward the target. This should move your left shoulder to the left and place your target approximately in line with your chest. Distribute your weight evenly for good balance.

Proper foot position

GRIP. If you're shooting a recurve bow, use a straight wrist grip, which puts the bow hand in the same position as if you were pointing at the target with your forefinger. This grip also keeps the bow arm and the arrow on the same direct plane to the target.

A low wrist grip does not work well for instinctive shooting because the bow arm and the arrow are not pointing together. A good technique for finding the correct grip is to point the bow hand, with forefinger extended, and place the bow between the thumb and forefinger.

Historically, longbows are shot with the heel of the bow hand down on the handle. Because the arrow and hand are not pointed together, as they are with the straight wrist grip, shooting the longbow is somewhat more difficult than shooting the recurve, and requires more practice.

DRAWING THE BOW. A stiff-arm swing draw is best for instinctive shooting, because it ensures a consistent shoulder position, which is crucial to accurate shooting.

When shooting a recurve bow, hold the bow with a straight wrist grip. Position the bow arm to the front and side of the forward leg, pointing straight toward the ground with the elbow in a locked position. When shooting a longbow, hold the bow with a heel-down hand position. In starting position, with the bow hand to the front and side of the forward leg, the elbow should form a natural curve.

Place the string in the outermost joint of the three drawing fingers, so they feel relaxed and secure.

Keeping the back of the hand relaxed, begin the draw. Swing the bow up and draw with a single motion, keeping your elbow and wrist straight. Bend your knees slightly as you draw; this will focus and intensify your concentration, and provide better alignment with your target. Make sure to draw using the muscles of your upper back, not the arm and shoulder; at full draw you should feel your upper back muscles under tension.

With instinctive shooting, the bow is slanted, or *canted* to the right or left as you shoot, depending on whether you are right- or left-handed. Canting the bow brings the eye closer and more in line with the arrow and rotates the upper part of the bow out of the line-of-sight, giving you a clearer picture of your target.

Pushing and pulling the bow simultaneously, maintaining proper back tension, is primary to all bow shooting and is the single most important ingredient in developing proficiency. The bow hand pushes toward the target as the bow arm pulls back, and this constant tension must be maintained throughout the shot. Without it, consistent accuracy is difficult to achieve.

Proper Grip for Shooting Recurves and Longbows

STRAIGHT WRIST GRIP is used with the recurve bow. At full draw, all pressure is between the thumb and the forefinger.

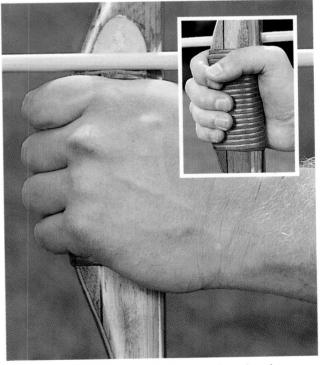

LOW WRIST GRIP is standard form when shooting a longbow. Pressure should fall on the back edge of the heel of the hand (inset). Gripping the bow with too much of the heel on the handle can cause the bow to twist during release, leading to poor arrow flight.

How to Draw a Recurve

HOLD the bow with a straight wrist grip, with the bow arm to the front and side of the forward leg. The bow points straight toward the ground, and the elbow is locked. String is held in the outermost joint of the first three fingers, so they are relaxed and secure.

BEGIN the draw, keeping the back of the string hand relaxed.

CONTINUE to swing the bow up and draw with a single motion, keeping the elbow and wrist of your bow arm straight.

PUSH the bow hand toward the target while using your back muscles to pull your string hand back to the anchor point. Maintain this tension throughout the draw. Keeping your knees slightly bent can improve your concentration and focus.

ANCHORING. As you reach the anchor point, tilt your head slightly, bringing your eye directly over the arrow. Most instinctive shooters anchor with the middle finger at the corner of the mouth, but some anchor at a tooth, feeling that this anchor point is less likely to move than the corner of the mouth. Take care not to use your cheek or chin to help hold the draw – the anchor point is a reference point only. The draw is held entirely with the upper back muscles.

CORRECT ANCHOR POSITION places the string hand, head and bow hand in straight alignment. The arrow nock is typically anchored near the corner of the mouth, and the head is tilted slightly over the top of the arrow.

AIMING. Throughout the draw, anchor and release, keep your eyes and concentration focused on the target. Intense and uninterrupted concentration on a single spot is what instinctive shooting is all about, and its importance cannot be overemphasized. The more complete your concentration, the better you will shoot.

You can practice this skill during your daily routine by picking out the smallest spot on everything you see – a small water spot on your office desk, a cracked taillight on a vehicle in traffic, a small bird high in a tree. Through practice, some shooters develop the ability to assume an almost trancelike concentration prior to and during the shot.

RELEASE. Many bow shooters worry needlessly about the release. After a few shots, beginners generally find that releasing the arrow is not as tricky as they fear. Done correctly, the release is a simple matter of relaxing of the fingers, as opposed to consciously turning loose. If the bow is drawn correctly – with the bow hand pushed toward the target and the string hand pulled back with the upper back muscles, the release will almost certainly be clean.

At release, your bow arm should spring slightly forward and remain pointed at the target, and the release hand should move slightly backward. This follow-through must be maintained until the arrow hits the target. Without correct follow-through, the bow arm may drop before the release, affecting the shot.

Don't force yourself to shoot too quickly. Many archers think that instinctive shooting means drawing and releasing quickly, and that it is incorrect to take your time. Allow your shot to develop its own rhythm and speed. Although it's true that an instinctive shooter usually begins to shoot somewhat quicker as his skills develop, speed is a result of experience, not a goal in itself. With instinctive shooting, the shot is made when your intuition says, "Now is the time."

Learning Good Instinctive Shooting

In my experience, a great many instinctive archers are shooting bows that are simply too stiff for them. By far the biggest impediment to learning good instinctive shooting is using a bow with too much draw weight. That's lesson number 1: select a bow you can draw and hold comfortably under any conditions. All the skills and mechanics of instinctive shooting can be mastered in only a few sessions – but only if you're able to draw and hold your bow easily.

With practice, instinctive shooting becomes 10 percent mechanical and 90 percent mental. When you begin, mechanics dominate, but as you gain experience, you'll find yourself concentrating more and more on the target as good form becomes automatic.

One way to develop the ability to concentrate on a single spot is to use a practice target with a single white spot painted on a large black background. If you become accustomed to focusing your attention this way, your accuracy when hunting in the field will also improve.

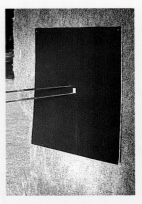

– Fred Asbell

Controlling
Target Panic

When you run into a bowhunter who says he never misses a shot, it's likely he's not telling you the whole truth. For one reason or another, all hunters – even experts – miss more critical shots than they care to admit. A few errant arrows are inevitable and should be accepted as part of the sport – as long as the reason for each miss is identified and understood. But the cause of missed shots is too often misdiagnosed. Archers often blame either their shooting ability or their equipment for a miss, when the real cause is panic or nervousness. Fiddling with equipment and taking more target practice won't solve this dilemma, because the archer hasn't focused on the real problem.

Diagnosing Target Panic

Target panic is the condition in which nervousness or excitement spoils a shot that is otherwise well within the archer's skill level. Among hunters, the condition is also known as *buck fever* – referring to the excitement that occurs when a hunter is faced with a large buck. For accurate shooting in pressure-packed hunting situations, controlling target panic is just as important as basic shooting skills and the ability to estimate distances. In most cases, target panic is the result of a hunter trying too hard. The condition is marked by flinching at the moment of release, snap shooting or freezing off the target.

For some shooters, target panic is a minor annoyance that occurs infrequently, but for others it can become a major problem. Some folks have target panic in all shooting situations – even when shooting alone in the backyard. Others may succumb to excitement only when a big buck is closing the distance, presenting the hunter with the shot of a lifetime. But no hunter is immune; sooner or later, everyone experiences some type of tension-related shooting problem.

Analyze every missed shot by asking yourself, "Would I have missed at that range if I was shooting at a target instead of an animal?" If your answer is yes, then more practice or a shorter shooting distance is the solution. But if the answer is no, then you probably need to start working to control a problem that is in your head, fed by nerves and excitement. Facing the problem and admitting it exists is the first step to a solution.

Methods for Controlling Target Panic

You can learn to focus and shoot with near your normal skill when faced with a pressure situation, but it requires mental toughness and a serious commitment. The following methods can all help you overcome pressure-related shooting problems; decide on one and dedicate yourself to it. When changing any aspect of your shooting routine, concentrate on getting the process right from the first arrow. Focus on shooting the arrow correctly, not on hitting a target or spot.

SHOOT A LIGHTER DRAW WEIGHT. Heavy-draw-weight bows add to physical tension and increase the likelihood of target panic. This is why compound bow shooters, who typically hold lower weights, have fewer panic-related shooting problems than longbow and recurve shooters. The first step to overcoming target panic is to practice with a bow with extremely light draw weight – 5 to 7 pounds, if you can find one.

PRACTICE "BLIND BALE" SHOOTING. Begin by standing very close, 5 yards or less, to a backstop. Don't set up a target; think only about shooting with correct form. It is helpful to close your eyes for several shots, but first make sure the area is safe and you have an observer nearby to watch for any potential hazards. Familiarize yourself with the feel of a perfect shot, without the distraction of aiming. Many experienced archers begin every target session with a few minutes of "blind bale" shooting.

Continue shooting into the backstop at close range until you feel your technique is solid and consistent. Once you are confident of your form, put up a target and practice shooting while increasing your distance in small increments. Always focus on shooting with correct form; tell yourself, "If I shoot this arrow correctly, I will hit the target." If you feel a loss of mental control at any point, start over again with the close-range practice.

THE BEST RELEASE AIDS for reducing target panic are those that discharge with back tension (above), or are operated with the thumb or pinkie finger.

Back-tension releases are available from:
Carter Enterprises
P.O. Box 19
St. Anthony, ID 83445

USE A RELEASE AID. Flinching and freezing often occur because a hunter anticipates the discharge of his bow. For those shooting compound bows, a mechanical release aid makes it more difficult to anticipate the discharge, and for this reason, a hunter prone to target panic can often control the problem by choosing the right release aid.

The best release aids for shooters fighting target panic are those that are triggered by increasing back pressure, not by consciously depressing a trigger with the index finger. Anticipation and flinching seem to appear more quickly and more severely when an index-finger style release aid is used, probably because the sensitivity and quick reaction time of the index finger make it more difficult to keep the discharge a surprise. Trigger-style releases discharged with thumb or pinkie finger may provide good long-term results, because they help do away with anticipation.

USE A CLICKER. The clicker is a device that signals the archer by making a soft, audible clicking sound at the instant it is time to release the arrow. Although clickers are generally recommended for finger-release shooters, some release-aid shooters, especially those who use index-finger styles, can also use clickers successfully.

CLICKERS for hunting setups must not interfere with the broadhead. The style shown here attaches to the upper limb of the bow and then to the bow-string. It works equally well with compounds, recurves and longbows.

Clicker are available from:
Clickety Klick
c/o Terry Arrow Rest
117 N. Pitt Street
Manheim, PA 17545

Clickers help control target panic, forcing you to focus on your form rather than on the cause of your nervousness – the animal. You must train yourself to draw to an exact draw length and wait for the signal to shoot. In addition, clickers require that you draw the bow another 1/8 inch while aiming. This gives good back tension, facilitating a better release.

Many expert hunters use clickers on all types of bows with both mechanical and finger releases and report no noise-related problems, but if you have doubts, the clicker's noise can be reduced by adding a piece of tape to the spring steel portion.

Many world-class competition archers use clickers, but these clicker styles generally don't work for hunting setups, because they interfere with broadheads. Make sure to choose a clicker made specifically for hunting.

Adapting to a New Style

Controlling target panic requires a dedicated shooter willing to experiment and adapt to new methods. For the best results, begin your work in the off season. Pick one of the methods described and commit to it seriously. Focus on getting your technique correct from the beginning; a rushed or halfhearted effort may do more harm than good.

For your first trip to the field after adapting a new method of shooting, it's best to start with small-game hunting. Shooting a few smaller animals in real hunting situations can help build your confidence in the new shooting technique.

Poor shooting diminishes the quality and enjoyment of the hunt. It can lead to wounded game and loss of confidence. But with a proper mental commitment you can perform under the inevitable pressure of hunting big game with a bow. Don't let your natural excitement work against you. Instead, talk to yourself and funnel that excitement toward the ultimate goal – shooting the arrow correctly. Then you will succeed.

Tuning

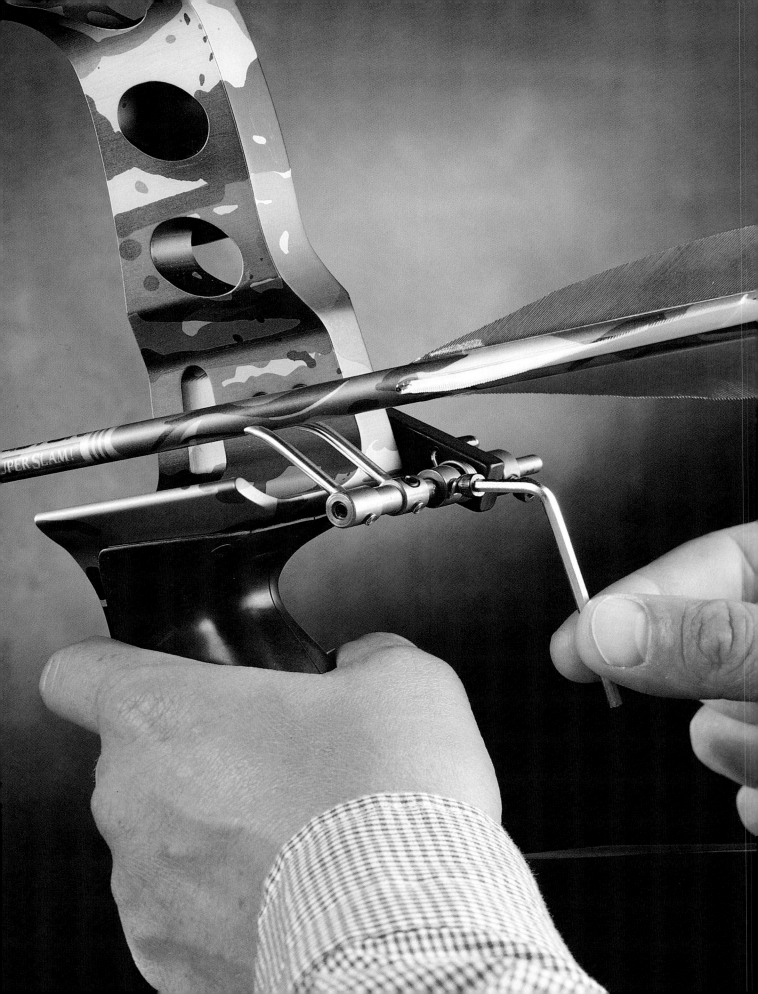

Tuning a Compound Bow

A compound bow must be periodically tested and adjusted. A well-tuned bow will shoot arrows with consistently true flight – the single most important prerequisite for ensuring accuracy and good penetration. You'll have little hope of getting the most from your compound bow unless you first tune it for true flight.

Tuning a bow involves three steps: the initial setup of the bow, testing arrow flight by shooting through paper, and making mechanical adjustments to correct problems. The tuning process can be complicated, requiring a gradual trial-and-error process. By isolating key variables and making the necessary adjustments, you can usually attain good performance. Make sure you are tuning with the same shooting methods and gear you'll be using in hunting situations. Any change in release style, grip or equipment will require that you recheck the bow's tune.

Setting Up Your Bow

DETERMINE PROPER ARROWS. Before you can fine-tune your compound bow, you'll need to make sure you're using arrows that are properly spined for your bow. Your selection of shafts will depend on your bow's poundage and your draw length, on the precise arrow length and on the weight of the points you'll be using. See "Arrows & Heads" (p. 32) for information on selecting arrows with the proper spine.

LIMB TILLER is the distance between the string and the bow limbs, measured at the point where the limb meets the riser. To adjust the tiller on one limb, turn the weight adjustment bolt: counterclockwise to increase the tiller; clockwise to decrease the tiller. One-cam bows (p. 13) do not need to be tillered. Simply crank the adjustment bolts in or out an equal amount.

SET THE TILLER. The limb tiller is the distance between the bowstring and each limb, measured at the point where each limb meets the riser (above). On many compound bows the tiller is set so the bottom limb is either even with the top limb, or slightly closer to the string than the top limb (no more than 1/8 inch). It's best to set the top and bottom tillers to the same distance. If the top and bottom tillers are not, the cams may turn over at different rates, which can cause irregular arrow flight.

ATTACH AND ADJUST THE ARROW REST. For best tuning, use an arrow rest that can be adjusted in and out (opposite page) to align the arrow with the bowstring – this adjustment is called the *center shot*.

The purpose of center-shot adjustment is to adjust the arrow rest so the arrow will be correctly aligned with the power stroke of the string. If you use a release aid, move the arrow rest to the left or right to position the arrow directly in line with the string. But if you are a finger-release shooter, the rest should be adjusted so you can just see the end of the arrow to the left side of the string (or the right side, if you're a left-handed archer). This adjustment compensates for the inevitable tendency of the string to push the arrow to one side when released with fingers. Refer to the rest manufacturer's instructions for specifics on how to make center-shot adjustments.

ATTACH THE NOCK SET. On two-cam bows, the nock set should be attached to the string so it is level with or 1/4 inch higher than the arrow rest, which is considered normal. Be sure to consider the diameter of the arrow shaft when positioning the nock set. If

you shoot with a release aid, use at least two nock sets to prevent them from slipping.

ROTATE ARROW NOCKS. For best flight, contact between an arrow's fletching and the arrow rest should be minimized. To check for this, spray a deodorant powder on the arrow shaft, fletching and rest, then take a test shot and look for disturbances in the powder on the arrow, indicating contact between the arrow, fleching and the rest. Some minor contact between the rest and the arrow shaft is inevitable, but fletching contact can be reduced simply by turning the nock slightly on the arrow shaft. With new arrows, it is best not to glue the nocks in place until you have determined the exact position for best fletching clearance. Some arrow nocks can be adjusted without removing them from the arrow.

CENTER-SHOT ADJUSTMENT positions the arrow rest so the arrow is either in straight alignment with the string (for release-aid shooters, left), or just to the side of the string (finger-release shooters, right).

DEODORANT POWDER can by sprayed on the arrow rest, arrow and fletching. When you release the arrow, powder residue will be disturbed, telling you how much contact there is between the arrow and the rest.

How to Attach Arrow Nock

ATTACH the nock set to the string so it is level with the arrow rest, or slightly higher. Use a T-square (also called a bow square) attached to the arrow string, and put the horizontal bar on the arrow rest.

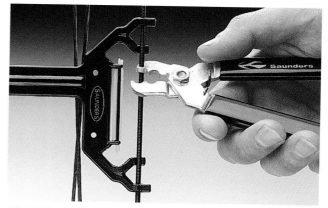

PLACE nock on string in the proper position, and apply pressure with nocking pliers to secure the nock to the string.

Build your own frame for a paper test, using cardboard; for safety, be sure to have a good backstop behind the frame

Testing Your Bow

In theory, a bow that has been set up carefully should require little tuning, but in practice this is rarely the case. The conventional method for testing a bow setup is to shoot arrows through sheets of paper at close range – 2 to 20 yards. Metal frames are available to hold sheets of paper, or you can make your own frame simply by cutting a window in the side of a cardboard box and taping a sheet of paper over the window. For safety, position a target bale about one yard behind the paper.

Some archers test with bare shafts with no fletching, but bare shafts can be very erratic in flight, which could cause arrow damage. Also, bare-shaft tests shouldn't be done with broadheads. Arrows that are fletched can be tested with broadheads and will provide a realistic test. Again, use the same shafts you will hunt with, and make sure they are correctly spined for your bow.

Take your first test shot from 2 to 5 yards from the paper. Concentrate on using a good, relaxed shooting form, not on aiming the bow.

If your bow is improperly tuned, as is likely when you begin paper tests, the arrow will wobble in flight and tear the paper at an angle, rather than a perfect bullet hole. Inspecting the paper target and interpret-

ing the direction of the tear will give clues as to how the bow needs to be adjusted to bring it into tune. Left or right tears indicate that the arrow is wobbling back and forth, a motion called *fishtailing*. Upward or downward tears indicate up and down motion, called *porpoising*.

Vertical wobbles may be the easist to diagnose and correct, but horizontal wobbles are more difficult to evaluate. Moving the arrow rest right or left should change the direction of the tear; a finger-release shooter may need a different adjustment than will a release-aid shooter. Adjusting for horizontal wobbles is a trial-and-error process: move the rest in one direction, and if the tear pattern doesn't improve, adjust the rest the other way until you achieve a satisfactory tear. If a good tear is not reached, other factors (p. 113) may be affecting the paper test.

The process of tuning your bow is a matter of gradually making small adjustments to the bow until the paper test shows a relatively smooth bullet hole. Don't expect to achieve perfect tune with a single adjustment. And don't insist on perfect arrow flight, especially at close range. A tear of 1/2 to 3/4 inch in addition to the shaft and fletching is perfectly acceptable. Attempting to achieve a perfect bullet hole may prove futile and unnecessarily lead to frustration.

After your bow is tuned at point-blank range, check it back to 20 yards, hoping that it gets better. At 20 yards you should have a near-perfect tear. Once your bow exhibits an excellent paper test at this distance, your bow can be considered well tuned and should shoot accurately. Now you're ready to sight-in the bow.

Paper Tear Patterns Indicating Arrow Flight

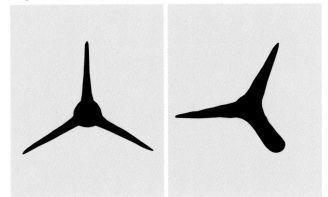

PROBLEM: Tail-down tear. *Possible solutions:* Move nock set up on string; strengthen the launcher arm.

PERFECT TUNE is represented by a paper test with a single "bullet hole" (left) with no rough tears. Clean slits radiating from the bullet hole show where the vanes or feathers have sliced through the paper. In practice, perfection is difficult to achieve. A paper test with a ½- to ¾-inch tear – high and to the left for right-handed shooters (right), and high and to the right for left-handed shooters – is often acceptable.

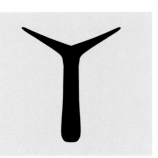

PROBLEM: Tail-up tear. *Possible solutions:* Move nock set down on string; weaken the launcher arm.

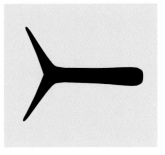

PROBLEM: Tail-left tear. *Possible solutions:* Increase spring tension in cushion plunger; move arrow rest horizontally; decrease bow weight; use stiffer arrows; shoot with mechanical aid; use shorter arrows, if possible.

PROBLEM: Tail-right tear. *Possible solutions:* Decrease spring tension in the cushion plunger; move rest horizontally; increase bow weight; use arrows with weaker spines; use longer arrows.

Common Adjustments for Incorrect Arrow Flight

ADJUSTING SPRING TENSION in the cushion plunger corrects right or left tears.

MOVING THE ARROW REST horizontally corrects left or right paper tears.

CHANGING NOCK SET POSITION should correct up-and-down tears.

Other Considerations

If you find it difficult or impossible to achieve true arrow flight, it is possible that the problem lies in your form or choice of equipment. If significant arrow flight problems persist despite your attempt at tuning, consider the following changes.

Analyze and change your form. Poor or inconsistent form can make it difficult to tune your bow. By analyzing your shooting style and form completely (p. 81), you can often solve arrow flight problems. Some finger-release shooters introduce an S-curve to the bowstring because of the way they anchor at full draw. Draw your bow while standing in front of a mirror (without an arrow) and look for string twist, a common error that can lead to erratic arrow flight for finger shooters. If you have severe twist, try dropping the top or bottom finger as you reach full draw. Many archers find that this method improves arrow flight.

An improper or inconsistent hand position on the grip can cause torque, disrupting the effectiveness of an otherwise well-tuned bow. Your hand must consistently be in the proper position to yield the best possible arrow flight.

EXPERIMENT WITH DIFFERENT ARROWS. Arrow shaft manufacturers usually have specific arrow guidelines for bows, but these recommendations may not work for every shooter and setup. You may find that using arrows with a different spine value can make your bow easier to tune.

CHANGE FLETCHING. If shooting with vanes, consider switching to feathers, which are more forgiving.

CHECK WHEEL SYNCHRONIZATION AND LIMB DEFLECTION. Cams that roll over at different rates can cause arrows to fly erratically. Checking wheel synchronization and limb deflection usually requires the services of a competent bow technician.

USE AN ELIMINATOR BUTTON. If you use a mechanical release aid, an eliminator button (right) can make the discharge smoother and improve arrow flight by cushioning the arrow between the nock set and the release aid.

CHANGE BOWS. Certain bow features can make tuning difficult. Low brace height, short axle-to-axle length, radical cams, overdraws and high arrow speeds can all make tuning difficult. If you find it impossible to tune your bow, you many want to try a different bow altogether.

CRITIQUE your shooting by videotaping it. You can evaluate the tape yourself, or show it to an experienced, knowledgeable shooter if you are unsure.

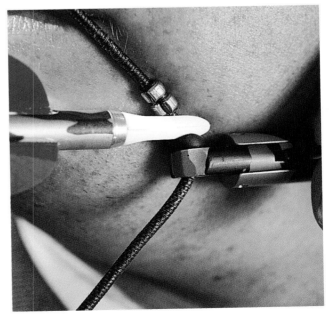

Eliminator button

RECURVE BOWS are usually center shot – they typically have a cutout area on the handle that allows the arrow to be aligned with the centerline of the bow (left). Longbows, by contrast, are non-center shot – the arrow rests to the side of the centerline on the bow handle (right).

HISTORICAL NOTE: The term "fistmele" comes from a medieval word meaning "fist measure," a method for gauging string height. Fistmele is measured by placing the base of the fist on the bow grip and extending the thumb. When braced according to the fistmele measurement, the brace height is about 6 to 7 inches.

Tuning Traditional Bows

RECURVE BOWS. Compared to a compound bow, a recurve bow is relatively easy to tune. There are only three adjustments you can make when shooting a recurve: changing the brace height, moving the nocking point and changing the arrows you shoot.

Begin by setting the brace height of your bow to the manufacturer's recommendations, then shoot it several times, noting how the bow feels and how the arrows fly. If the bow is too noisy, or has excessive vibration, it means that the brace height is too low.

To increase the brace height, use a bowstringer (p. 31) to detach the string from one limb, then shorten the string by twisting it two or three times before

ADJUST the brace height on a traditional bow by twisting or untwisting the bowstring. Twisting increases the brace height, while untwisting decreases the brace height.

reattaching it. Now take a few more shots to get the feel of the bow and check arrow flight. Continue this process of shooting the bow and shortening the string until you reach the ideal brace height – the point where vibrations and noise diminish. Don't shorten the string too far; although this has little effect on arrow flight, it will make your bow draw harder. If your bow is drawing too hard, you can decrease the brace height by untwisting the string.

While testing, use a temporary nocking point (opposite page), such as a piece of tape positioned just above the arrow. To find this point, use a T-square with the horizontal leg placed on the arrow rest and the vertical leg attached to the string. Start by positioning the nocking point 3/8 inch above the point where the horizontal leg touches the string. Shoot

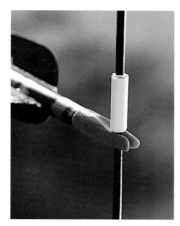

Use tape for a temporary nocking point

several test arrows. If the nocking point is too low or too high, the arrow will fly in an erratic up-and-down "porpoise" motion. After you have arrived at the optimum brace height and have found a nocking position that eliminates porpoising, then install a permanent nock set.

Selecting the correct arrow for your recurve bow is important, but fairly simple. Recurve bows are typically center shot, with a handle cutout that positions the arrow in direct line with the center of the bow. Because the power stroke of the string propels the arrow straight forward with little fishtailing, you have a fairly large leeway when choosing arrows. Arrow charts (pp. 34-36) can help you choose arrows. You can also take your bow to a good archery shop, stocked with a wide variety of arrows, and let their professionals help you determine the best arrow for your bow through trial and error. This will also save the expense of buying the many arrows needed to check for best arrow flight.

LONGBOWS. The longbow is even less temperamental than the recurve bow and is very simple to set up. The most common problem for longbow shooters is bad arrow flight, which typically occurs because the arrows are not correctly matched to the bow. Longbow shooters are often advised that their bows require heavier-spine arrows, but this is not the case.

Because a longbow is not center shot, an arrow must bend and flex as it goes around the bow handle in order to fly straight to the target. This bending is popularly known as *arrow paradox*, but is more properly called *archer's paradox*. The best arrow

ENLIST the help of a friend when checking for proper arrow flight. It is difficult to watch the flight while focusing on maintaining good shooting form.

for a longbow is often much lighter in spine than the appropriate arrow for a comparable recurve bow, because lighter-spine arrows bend around the bow handle more easily. Selecting the arrow and matching it to the bow are critical to consistent shooting with a longbow.

As with recurves, set the brace height to manufacturer's recommendations. Then shoot several times to see how the arrow flies; if the bow is noisy or vibrates excessively, the brace height may need to be adjusted by twisting the string.

Arrow straightness is crucial when shooting a non-center shot bow, such as the longbow, because a crooked arrow will not bend evenly as it leaves the bow.

Effects of Archers Paradox

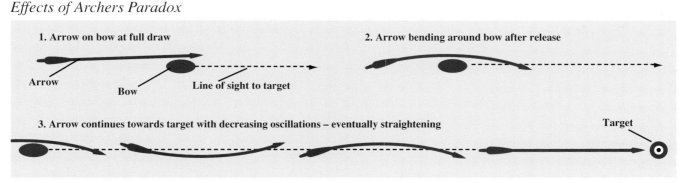

ARCHER'S PARADOX is the action of the arrow bending around the bow handle under the pressure of the released bowstring.

FIELD POINT		BROADHEAD
5"		4"
3"		4"
6"		5"
2"		3"
3"		3"
+ 19"		+ 19"
5		5
3.8"		3.8"

Tuning for Broadheads

The goal of any bowhunter is superior broadhead accuracy and excellent arrow flight. All our effort, our experimenting and bow adjustments should be aimed at these objectives. But most bowhunters get so wrapped up in tuning that they neglect the final and most crucial test – broadhead accuracy. The overall accuracy of your broadheads, as determined by measuring the size of arrow groups, should be nearly as good as it is for field-point groups.

Don't confuse broadhead accuracy with whether your broadheads and field points hit in the same place (point of impact). These are separate and distinct issues and will be treated individually in this section. Far and away, the broadhead accuracy question is the more important of the two. It should be the final check before you are completely satisfied and ready to hunt.

Many bowhunters assume that broadheads and field points will automatically strike in the same place, so long as they weigh the same. Although identical point weights do ensure that overall arrow weights and spine (stiffness) are the same, this doesn't mean arrow grouping will be identical. Unlike target points, the blades of a broadhead compete with the fletches for control of the arrow. Consequently,

arrows equipped with broadheads may well perform differently from those equipped with target points.

Point-of-Impact

Sometimes, the initial tuning adjustments will do the trick and your broadheads and field points will hit in the same place. When this happens, count your blessings and move on to the arrow-group test. But if it's not the case, don't despair. Often, a few minor tuning adjustments can help you achieve nearly identical sight settings for field points and broadheads, particularly at close range.

To test for impact point, begin by shooting both broadheads and field points into a broadhead target, and look for differences in the location of arrow groups.

HORIZONTAL ADJUSTMENTS. If your broadheads tend to hit to the right or left of the field points, adjust the center shot (your arrow rest) horizontally until the arrow groups come together. Because there are so many variables in shooting styles and release methods, this adjustment should be regarded as a trial-and-error process: make small adjustments until you get satisfactory results.

VERTICAL ADJUSTMENTS. If your broadheads hit higher than your field points, move the nocking point up slightly; if your broadheads hit lower, move the nocking point down.

Continue to shoot both types of heads and make small adjustments until the broadheads and field points hit as close as possible. Then, conduct a final check at your maximum effective shooting range. The greater the distance, the finer your adjustments will need to be.

Don't worry if your broadheads refuse to strike precisely the same spot as your field points, but if you can't get them to strike reasonably close, you may want to consider using a different broadhead style, such as a high-quality, open-on-impact head.

Testing Broadhead Accuracy

Once the point-of-impact issue has been settled (even if it was not to your complete satisfaction), proceed with a broadhead accuracy test. The materials you need include: a pencil, paper for a score sheet, a ruler, a good broadhead target and four arrows in perfect condition, two equipped with field points and two with broadheads. Make two columns on the score sheet, marking one "FP" for field-point and one "BH" for broadhead.

From your maximum effective range, shoot the four arrows at the broadhead target five to ten times. To make the test as fair as possible, be sure to alternate between field points and broadheads. Don't make any sight adjustments as long as the arrows are hitting safely within the target, because you're only interested in comparing the distances between arrows of the same type. After shooting each group, measure the distance between the two broadhead arrows and record the result in the appropriate column on the score sheet; then do the same for the two field points. A colored mark on the nocks of one of the arrow sets can help you distinguish between the types when the heads are buried in the target.

From the beginning, be sure to watch for a "flier" arrow – one that consistently strikes away from the others. If you spot such an arrow, replace it and start the test over from the beginning.

After shooting and recording several arrow groups, add the columns separately and divide them by the number of times you shot. This will give you the average group size for each arrow type.

Although top-quality, average-size broadheads are capable of the same tight accuracy as field points, some bows that shoot accurately with field points are intolerant of broadheads. If the average group size for your broadheads is more than 1 inch larger than the average group for your practice points, you may have an accuracy problem requiring some adjustments and retuning specifically for shooting broadheads.

When you find your broadhead grouping to be consistently tight, make the final sight adjustments to get the arrows to the desired impact point. Further

PLACE a colored mark on the nocks of one arrow type to distinguish between broadheads and field-points when the heads are buried in the target.

practice with broadheads will improve your confidence and prepare you to deliver an accurately placed arrow in real hunting situations.

If your broadheads still do not group well after making these adjustments, you may need to revisit basic tuning procedures (p. 109). The following tips may also help.

• CHECK to make sure nocks and broadheads are perfectly aligned with the shaft (pp. 40 and 43).

• CHANGE to broadheads with smaller blades, or with vented blades. Or try a high-quality, open-on-impact style broadhead (pp. 42 and 43).

• REPLACE vanes with feather fletching (p. 40).

• REDUCE draw weight slightly.

• TRY helical fletched arrows (p. 41).

• ALIGN the fletching with the blades, if you use three-blade broadheads with three-fletch arrows.

• CHECK the arrow's balance point. Ten percent or more forward of center is best (p. 43-44).

• MEASURE the size, weight and length of all your arrows to make sure they are consistent (p. 33). Small variations in arrows can create marked differences in performance.

Kinetic Energy

WITH MODERN COMPOUND BOWS, lighter draw weights can achieve sufficient kinetic energy to take large game.

The killing force of an arrow is determined largely by its kinetic energy, a measurement based on the speed and weight of the arrow. For the bowhunter, kinetic energy is important as a measurement of an arrow's penetrating ability. The higher the kinetic energy of your arrows, the greater their killing power. Keep kinetic energy in mind when choosing a setup for the hunt.

MEASURING KINETIC ENERGY. The formula used to compute kinetic energy is: $[(V^2 \times W) \div 450,240]$.

First, multiply the velocity of the arrow in feet per second times itself: $(V \times V)$. For an arrow traveling 250 feet per second, for example, the velocity squared is 62,500.

Then, multiply this number times the weight (W) of the arrow, in grains. For a 450-grain arrow, this calculation for our example equals 28,125,000: $(250^2) \times 450$.

Finally, divide this number by 450,240 to arrive at the kinetic energy in foot-pounds. In our example, the result is 62.466 foot-pounds: $28,125,000 \div 450,240$.

Obviously, few archers have access to a chronograph, which is necessary to measure velocity. For this reason, manufacturers' organizations provide buyers with bow speed ratings which can be used to compare bows. The Archery Manufacturers and Merchants Organization (AMO) bow speed ratings are determined using 60 pounds draw weight, a 30-inch draw length and 540-grain arrows. The IBO speed ratings are determined with arrows that weigh 5 grains for each pound of draw weight. Although these ratings offer a valuable method for comparing bows, the numbers are only approximations.

Your actual velocity will vary if your bow is set to a different draw weight, or if you have a different draw length or if you shoot a different arrow weight. If you want precise velocity measurements for your arrows, some bow shops have chronographs and will measure your arrow speed for a small fee.

DRAW WEIGHT AND KINETIC ENERGY. In the past, when it was assumed that kinetic energy and killing power were determined exclusively by draw weight, hunters were advised to use specific draw weights for big game – 50 pounds for deer, 60 pounds for elk, for example – and many states still have laws that prescribe minimum draw weights. In the days before compound bows, this standard made some sense, because all bows had similar performance levels.

But modern compound bows make those guidelines irrelevant, since two bows with the same draw weight can vary enormously in their efficiency and speed. A 60-pound longbow, for example, can shoot a 540-grain arrow at about 180 fps, generating about 37.8 foot-pounds of kinetic energy. On the other hand, a cam bow with an identical 60-pound draw weight can have a speed rating of 240 fps or higher, generating almost 65 foot-pounds of kinetic energy – more than enough to kill the largest game animals.

In addition to bow design, other factors can influence arrow speed and kinetic energy. Draw length and bow length, for example, both have a direct influence on kinetic energy. A bow with a 32-inch draw length at 60 pounds has a longer power stroke and will shoot considerably faster than a bow with a 26-inch draw length; this is why the AMO uses a standard 30-inch draw length when rating bows. Shorter axle-to-axle bows also are generally faster than longer bows. Finally, the type of string can also make a difference. A nonstretching Fast Flight or Vectran string will shoot faster than a Dacron string, which stretches.

ARROW WEIGHT AND KINETIC ENERGY. In an effort to wring the most kinetic energy out of each shot, many archers use ultralight, ultrafast arrows. But while lightweight arrows are indeed fast, they do not necessarily carry more kinetic energy and killing power. Although a heavier arrow shot from the same bow does fly slower, it also carries more momentum and therefore more kinetic energy. When choosing a setup, remember that kinetic energy is the key number, not sheer arrow speed.

In reality, lightning-fast arrow speeds are rarely necessary with today's modern compound bows. A deer can be easily killed with an arrow carrying 40 foot-pounds of kinetic energy, and elk and other large game can be taken with an arrow delivering 50 foot-pounds. These levels are easily attainable with mediumweight arrows, as shown in the chart (right).

In fact, heavier arrows have several advantages over ultralight arrows. For one thing, they are more stable and forgiving than light arrows. Because they absorb more of the bow's energy, heavy arrows reduce vibration in the bow limbs. Shooting ultralight arrows, by contrast, can seriously stress your bow, much the way dry-firing does. Finally, many hunters feel that a slightly heavier arrow packs more penetration power than an extremely light arrow, possibly because the arrow oscillates less in flight.

With a modern compound bow, a good rule of thumb is to strive for a combination of draw weight and arrow weight that provides 40 to 50 foot-pounds of kinetic energy – a force that will drive an arrow completely through a large game animal. Shooting with a setup that delivers 70 or 80 foot-pounds of kinetic energy is simply not necessary, and is difficult for many hunters to handle.

Comparison of Feet Per Second to Kinetic Energy

AMO rating	Kinetic energy	IBO rating	Kinetic energy
190 fps	43.30	240 fps	38.38
195 fps	45.60	245 fps	40.00
200 fps	47.97	250 fps	41.64
190 fps	50.40	255 fps	43.33
205 fps	52.89	260 fps	45.04
210 fps	58.04	265 fps	46.79
220 fps	60.72	270 fps	48.57
225 fps	63.45	275 fps	50.39
230 fps	66.23	280 fps	52.24
235 fps	69.08	285 fps	54.12
240 fps	71.99	290 fps	56.07
250 fps	74.96	295 fps	57.9
255 fps	77.99	300 fps	59.96

SPEED RATINGS can help you determine the approximate kinetic energy of your bow. The AMO chart (left) assumes a 540-grain arrow shot from a 60-pound bow with a 30-inch draw length. The IBO chart (right) presumes an arrow that weighs 5 grains per pound of draw weight; numbers listed here presume a 60-pound draw weight and 300-grain arrow.

Kinetic Energy Ratings

		AMO Velocity Rating in Feet Per Second (FPS)								
		190	200	210	220	230	240	250	260	270
Arrow Weight in Grains	300	24	27	29	32	35	38	42	45	49
	325	26	29	32	35	38	42	45	49	53
	350	28	31	34	38	41	45	49	53	57
	375	30	33	37	40	44	48	52	56	61
	400	32	36	39	43	47	51	56	60	65
	425	34	38	42	46	50	54	59	64	69
	450	36	40	44	48	53	58	62	68	73
	475	38	42	47	51	56	61	66	71	77
	500	40	44	49	54	59	64	69	75	81
	525	42	47	51	56	62	67	73	79	85
	550	44	48	54	59	65	70	76	83	89
	575	48	51	56	62	68	74	80	86	93
	600	50	53	59	64	70	77	83	90	97

KINETIC ENERGY RATINGS are based on arrow weight and arrow velocity. When changing total arrow weight, you will need to adjust the bow poundage in order to achieve the same kinetic energy.

Self-Tuning

You've carefully chosen a good bow and quality accessories, and you have tuned your equipment as precisely as possible. You've mastered the basic skills of shooting a bow and arrow, and you've practiced until you can consistently place practice arrows within an 8-inch group at your maximum shooting range. Nothing left to do; you're ready to bring home a record-book whitetail on opening day, right?

Not so fast. Proper equipment and good physical skills can take you only so far; after that, successful bowhunting is mostly a mind game. Think about it; once you've mastered the basics of shooting a bow and arrow, once you've honed your practice skills to a satisfactory prehunt sharpness, what else can be done to prepare yourself for that pulse-pounding moment when a deer steps into a shooting lane near your stand? How can you develop the confidence and self-control necessary to deliver a broadhead-tipped arrow to an exact spot on your quarry's rib cage?

Real-life bowhunting situations are guaranteed to stir strong emotions in a hunter, nervous excitement that leads to target panic unless controlled (p. 103). Many highly skilled archers, deadly accurate when shooting at the target range, suddenly experience trembling hands, weak knees and shortness of breath at the mere sight of approaching antlers. Without the ability to control emotions during pressure-packed, face-to-face encounters with game animals, a hunter is almost certainly doomed to failure.

PRACTICE, using the same clothes and accessories you will be using when hunting. This allows you to grow accustomed to hunting conditions, increasing your confidence.

Self-tuning is the process of learning to control emotion while hunting. It is accomplished by developing two traits essential to bowhunting success: self-confidence and self-control. A few bowhunters are blessed with both traits from birth, but for most of us it is not so simple. Fortunately, self-confidence and self-control are skills that can be developed using specific techniques. It takes considerable effort, however, and it can't be done overnight.

Proper Practice

Confidence in your own skills can be improved by making your target practice sessions as realistic as possible. Carry the same equipment and wear the same clothes during practice that you will use when hunting. If you plan to wear a camouflage face mask or gloves while hunting, wear these articles while practicing. If you'll be hunting from an elevated

SHOOT from the same stance and position, when practicing, as you will when hunting. If you will be hunting from a tree stand, for example, shoot extensively from a tree stand during your practice sessions.

Shoot 3-D targets or participate in organized shooting events that offer realistic targets or hunting situations

stand, practice shooting from an elevated stand (always wearing a safety belt). And, for practice, use the same broadhead-tipped arrows that you'll hunt with later (always replace the blades before you hunt).

Regular, frequent practice also helps build confidence. Shoot year-round, if possible. Join a local bowhunting club or league. Attend shoots, especially those offering realistic 3-D animal targets placed in hunting terrain. Establish a regular practice schedule that allows you to improve or maintain your accuracy. The goal is to repeat the physical act of drawing, anchoring, aiming, releasing and following through – arrow after arrow – until the process becomes routine, almost automatic. When you later face an actual hunting situation, you'll be able to shoot without worrying or even thinking about the steps necessary to draw and release an arrow.

In-the-Field Experience

Extensive target-range practice has its place, but nothing prepares you for bowhunting's moment of truth like hunting itself. Carry your bow each time you head afield. Stump-shooting at imaginary bucks

during preseason scouting trips to your hunting area is good practice. You should also be stalking and shooting varmints, small game or roughfish throughout the off-season. In this way, you begin to learn how to apply practice-session skills to real-life situations. Each arrow you release builds confidence and sets the stage for actual hunting experiences.

But don't neglect practice once the hunting season begins. Shoot at least one practice arrow from your stand each time you hunt. And on days when you're not in the field, make time to keep your shooting skills sharp. You'll find that this investment pays off when that moment of truth finally arrives.

Physical Conditioning

Regular shooting prepares the muscles needed to draw and release an arrow at a game animal, but typical practice sessions, no matter how frequent, do little to prepare you for the physical demands of hunting in the field. Walking to a tree stand near a road doesn't require great physical conditioning, but transporting a large buck out of the deep woods is another matter. And to adequately prepare for the rigors of an elk hunt at high elevations, you may need to put in many weeks of hard physical exercise. A once-in-a-lifetime hunting opportunity can be ruined if you don't have the strength and stamina to pursue game animals over rough terrain. If you don't believe physical conditioning is important, consider this fact: each year, some hunters die after suffering heart attacks while hunting.

Much has been written about fitness and the different strategies for getting into good physical shape, but the best advice is to find an exercise routine you find enjoyable – or at least tolerable. If you find running laps at a fitness club to be tedious, try jogging along country roads. Or, get into a routine of brisk hiking through the area where you'll be hunting; while getting in shape, you can also do preseason scouting.

Whatever exercise plan you follow, begin slowly to ensure that you don't injure yourself. Plan on exercising for 30 to 60 minutes a day, for a period of 4 to 8 weeks, depending on how much you need to improve your fitness. If it's been some time since you've exercised regularly, it's a good idea to get a physical exam before you start a fitness plan.

Visualization

Champion tournament archers don't just walk up to the line with a blank mind, pull back and hit the bullseye. Rather, they form a mental picture of the shot – drawing with perfect form, centering the sight on the target, releasing smoothly and seeing the arrow strike the target. This technique of mental imagery is called *visualization*, and elite tournament archers attribute their success as much to this mental training as to their physical skills.

Mental conditioning is even more valuable for bowhunters, since a hunter can't practice on live targets. You may get only one or two shots at a deer each year, hardly enough to develop a strong mental image, but with visualization, you can precondition yourself for this moment.

During your practice sessions, visualize yourself close to your buck. See his rippling muscles, hear his breathing, smell his musky glands, feel his presence. See yourself picking one hair behind his shoulder as your target and slowly raising your bow and drawing smoothly. See the sight pin settling on that hair behind his shoulder, feel the string smoothly slipping away, and watch the arrow strike precisely where you aimed it. Practice this mental routine over and over until it's an automatic, vivid response. Then, when you have a live deer at 20 yards, you'll be ready for the moment because you've already lived it dozens of times.

Putting it all together results in success

Self-Talk

Every human being conducts a continuous inner dialogue with himself – at a rate of 400 to 500 words per minute, in the estimation of some psychologists. The quality of this internal dialogue can have a major bearing on bowhunting performance. Negative self-talk can defeat you, but positive dialogue can make you a winner. During the hunt, constantly monitor your thoughts, mentally "turning off" negative comments and replacing them with positive messages. Never let yourself say things like, "I blew that last shot; I'll probably blow this one, too." Instead, talk to yourself positively. "I've been

shooting well. I'll concentrate on picking a spot and executing a perfect shot." Don't dismiss this technique as mental hocus-pocus. Positive self-talk is a self-fulfilling prophecy: if you expect to succeed, you will.

All successful bowhunters realize that thorough preparation – readying oneself mentally as well as physically – is an essential part of the hunting experience. Self-tuning is a process that may take many years, but hard work that fine-tunes the equipment, body and mind is the best path to consistent hunting success. As one veteran deer hunter puts it, "It seems the harder I work, the luckier I become."

Index

Contributing Photographers (Note: T=*Top*, C=*Center*, B=*Bottom*, L=*Left*, R=*Right*, I=*Inset*)

Charles J. Alsheimer
Bath, New York
© *Charles J. Alsheimer: pp. 11, 102-103, 120-121*

G. Fred Asbell
Longmont, Colorado
© *G. Fred Asbell: pp. 100TL, 100TR, 100BL, 100BR*

Dan Bertalan
East Lansing, Michigan
© *Dan Bertalan: p. 27BR*

The Green Agency
Bozeman, Montana
© *Dale C. Spartas: p. 91*

Mark Kayser
Pierre, South Dakota
© *Mark Kayser: cover*

Chris Kuehn
Brooklyn Park, Minnesota
© *Chris Kuehn: p. 123*

Stephen W. Maas
Wyoming, Minnesota
© *Stephen W. Maas: pp. 4, 118*

Dr. Dave Samuel
Morgantown, West Virginia
© *Dr. Dave Samuel: backcover TL*

Joseph L. Tieszen
Aberdeen, South Dakota
© *Joseph L. Tieszen: pp. 23BC, 105BR*

Contributing Manufacturers

Altier Archery Mfg.
P.O. Box 286
Honesdale, Pennsylvania 18431

Barrie Archery
P.O. Box 482
Waseca, Minnesota 56093

Bighorn Bowhunting Company
2709 West Eisenhower Boulevard
Loveland, Colorado 80537

BrackLynn Products Inc.
4400 Stillman Boulevard Suite C
Tuscaloosa, Alabama 35401

Carter Enterprises
P.O. Box 19
Saint Anthony, Idaho 83445

Easton Technical Products, Inc.
5040 West Harold Gatty Drive
Salt Lake City, Utah 84116

Fine-Line Inc.
11304-A Steele Street South
Lakewood, Washington 98499

Golden Key-Futura, Inc.
P.O. Box 1446
Montrose, Colorado 81402

Highlander Sports Inc.
3004 11th Avenue
Huntsville, Alabama 35805

Hoyt USA
543 North Neil Armstrong Road
Salt Lake City, Utah 84116

McKenzie Sports Products Inc.
P.O. Box 480
Granite Quarry, North Carolina 28072

Mathews Inc.
919 River Road P.O. Box 367
Sparta, Wisconsin 54656

Montana Black Gold
34370 East Frontage Road
Bozeman, Montana 59715

Mountaineer Archery, Inc.
4340 Terrace Avenue Bldg. 3-A
Huntington, West Virginia 25722

Muzzy Products Corp.
110 Beasley Road
Cartersville, Georgia 30120

Neet Products, Inc.
5875 East Highway 50
Sedalia, Missouri 65301

New Archery Products Corp.
7500 Industrial Drive
Forest Park, Illinois 60130

The North American Archery Group
4600 Southwest 41st Boulevard
Gainsville, Florida 32608

Precision Shooting Equipment, Inc.
2727 North Fairview
Tucson, Arizona 85705

Predator Inc.
2605 Coulee Avenue
LaCrosse, Wisconsin 54601

Realtree Products
1390 Box Circle
Columbus, Georgia 31907

Saunders Archery Co.
P.O. Box 476
Columbus, Nebraska 68601

Scott Archery Manufacturing, Inc.
P.O. Box 7
Henderson, Kentucky 42420

Sight Master
1093 Highway 12 East
Townsend, Montana 59644

Terry Arrow Rest
117 North Pitt Street
Manheim, Pennsylvania 17545

Zwickey Archery Inc.
2571 East 12th Avenue
North St. Paul, Minnesota 55109